Contenu

High-frequency words 4

Module 1
Words I should know for speaking and writing activities 15
Extra words I should know for reading and listening activities 18

Module 2
Words I should know for speaking and writing activities 19
Extra words I should know for reading and listening activities 22

Module 3
Words I should know for speaking and writing activities 23
Extra words I should know for reading and listening activities 26

Module 4
Words I should know for speaking and writing activities 27
Extra words I should know for reading and listening activities 30

Module 5
Words I should know for speaking and writing activities 31
Extra words I should know for reading and listening activities 34

Module 6
Words I should know for speaking and writing activities 35
Extra words I should know for reading and listening activities 38

Module 7
Words I should know for speaking and writing activities 40
Extra words I should know for reading and listening activities 43

Module 8
Words I should know for speaking and writing activities 44
Extra words I should know for reading and listening activities 47

High-frequency words

Common –er verbs

accepter	to accept
adorer	to love, to adore
aider	to help
aimer	to like
aller	to go
aller à pied	to walk
allumer	to light, to turn, to switch on
améliorer	to improve
(s)'arrêter	to stop

Had a look ☐ **Nearly there** ☐ **Nailed it** ☐

chanter	to sing
chercher	to look for
cliquer	to click (ICT)
coller	to stick
commander	to order
compter/compter sur	to count, to intend, to count on (someone)
contacter	to contact
continuer	to continue, to carry on
copier	to copy
se coucher	to go to bed
coûter	to cost

Had a look ☐ **Nearly there** ☐ **Nailed it** ☐

se débrouiller	to cope, to manage, to get by
décider	to decide
décoller	to take off (plane)
se dépêcher	to hurry
dépenser	to spend (money)
se déshabiller	to get undressed
désirer	to want, to desire
dessiner	to draw
détester	to hate
discuter	to discuss
donner	to give
durer	to last

Had a look ☐ **Nearly there** ☐ **Nailed it** ☐

s'échapper	to escape
écouter	to listen
écraser	to squash
empêcher	to prevent
endommager	to harm, to damage

entrer	to enter, to go in
envoyer	to send
espérer	to hope
essayer	to try
étudier	to study
expliquer	to explain

Had a look ☐ **Nearly there** ☐ **Nailed it** ☐

se fâcher	to get angry
fermer	to close, to switch off
frapper	to knock, to hit
gagner	to earn, to win
garder	to look after, to mind (child, dog)
garer	to park
gérer	to manage (business)
s'habiller	to get dressed
habiter	to live (inhabit)
informer	to inform
inviter	to invite
jeter	to throw

Had a look ☐ **Nearly there** ☐ **Nailed it** ☐

laisser	to leave behind (an object)
(se) laver	to wash
se lever	to get up
louer	to rent, to hire
manger	to eat
manquer	to miss, to be lacking
marcher	to walk, to work (function)
mériter	to deserve
monter	to climb, to get on(to), to go up
monter (dans)	to get into (bus, car, train)
montrer	to show
nettoyer	to clean
noter	to note

Had a look ☐ **Nearly there** ☐ **Nailed it** ☐

s'occuper de	to look after
organiser	to organise
ôter	to take off (clothes etc.)
oublier	to forget, to leave something behind
pardonner	to forgive
parler	to speak
passer	to pass, to spend (time)
penser	to think (about)

peser	to weigh
pleurer	to cry
porter	to wear
poser	to place
pousser	to push
préférer	to prefer
présenter	to introduce (a person), to present
prêter	to lend
se promener	to go for a walk
quitter	to leave (somewhere, somebody)

Had a look ☐ **Nearly there** ☐ **Nailed it** ☐

raconter	to tell, to recount
se rappeler	to remember
rater	to fail, to miss (train, bus, etc.)
rechercher	to research
recommander	to recommend
regretter	to regret, to be sorry
rembourser	to refund
remercier	to thank
remplacer	to replace
rencontrer	to meet
rentrer (à la maison)	to return (home), to go back (home)
renverser	to knock over
réparer	to repair
répéter	to repeat
se reposer	to rest
réserver	to reserve
ressembler	to look like, to resemble
rester	to stay
retourner (à l'école)	to return (to school), to go back (to school)
se réveiller	to wake up
rouler	to go (in a car)

Had a look ☐ **Nearly there** ☐ **Nailed it** ☐

sauter	to jump
sauver	to save
sembler	to seem
signer	to sign
signifier	to mean, to signify
sonner	to ring (a bell)
souhaiter	to wish
stationner	to park
téléphoner	to phone
(se) terminer	to end

tirer	to pull
tomber	to fall
toucher	to touch
travailler	to work
traverser	to cross, to go across
trouver	to find

Had a look ☐ **Nearly there** ☐ **Nailed it** ☐

utiliser	to use
vérifier	to check
voler	to fly, to steal
voyager	to travel

Had a look ☐ **Nearly there** ☐ **Nailed it** ☐

Common –ir verbs

atterrir	to land
choisir	to choose
s'endormir	to fall asleep
finir	to finish, to end
nourrir	to feed, to nourish
offrir	to offer, to give a present/gift
ouvrir	to open
partir	to leave, to depart
prévenir	to warn
remplir	to fill, to fill in
réussir	to succeed
se servir de	to use
sortir	to go out
se souvenir	to remember
tenir	to hold
venir	to come

Had a look ☐ **Nearly there** ☐ **Nailed it** ☐

Common –re verbs

apprendre	to learn
attendre	to wait for
boire	to drink
conduire	to drive
connaître	to know (person, place)
décrire	to describe
descendre (de)	to get out of (bus, car, train)
dire	to tell, to say
entendre	to hear
éteindre	to switch off
(se) faire mal	to hurt (oneself)
introduire	to introduce (an item, an idea)
lire	to read

Had a look ☐ **Nearly there** ☐ **Nailed it** ☐

mettre	to put	paresseux/-euse	lazy
plaire (à)	to please	(im)patient(e)	(im)patient
prendre	to take	pessimiste	pessimistic
produire	to produce	petit(e)	small, short (person)
remettre	to put back	(im)poli(e)	(im)polite
répondre	to reply	populaire	popular
rire	to laugh	responsable	responsible
sourire	to smile	rigolo(te)	funny (comical)
suivre	to follow	sage	good (well-behaved), wise
vivre	to live	sérieux/-euse	serious
vendre	to sell	sévère	strict
		strict(e)	strict

Had a look ☐ **Nearly there** ☐ **Nailed it** ☐

		sympa (invariable)	nice, likeable
		sympathique	nice, likeable
		timide	shy

Common –*oir* verbs

avoir	to have	travailleur/-euse	hard-working
avoir besoin de	to need	vilain(e)	naughty
avoir l'intention de (faire)	to mean to (do)		
devoir	to have to, to must		
savoir	to know (a fact)		
voir	to see		
vouloir	to want		

Had a look ☐ **Nearly there** ☐ **Nailed it** ☐

Common adjectives: I am, you are, we are …

célèbre	famous
content(e)	pleased
de bonne humeur	in a good mood
étonné(e)	surprised

Common adjectives: describing someone

actif/-ve	active	faible (en maths, etc.)	weak (in maths, etc.)
agréable	pleasant	fatigué(e)	tired
amical(e)	friendly	fort(e) (en maths, etc.)	strong (in maths, etc.)
bavard(e)	talkative	heureux/-euse	happy, content
bête	silly	inquiet/-iète	worried
calme	peaceful, quiet, calm	jeune	young
désagréable	unpleasant	malheureux/-euse	unhappy
drôle	funny (comical)	perdu(e)	lost
égoïste	selfish	pressé(e)	in a hurry
généreux/-euse	generous	reconnaissant(e)	grateful
gentil(le)	kind	riche	rich
gros(se)	fat	satisfait(e)	satisfied
honnête	honest	sauf/-ve	safe
indépendant(e)	independent	surpris(e)	surprised
intelligent(e)	intelligent, clever	triste	sad
joli(e)	pretty	vieux/vieil/vieille	old
laid(e)	ugly		
marrant(e)	funny (comical)		
méchant(e)	naughty		
mince	slim		

Had a look ☐ **Nearly there** ☐ **Nailed it** ☐ (opinions/describing)

Had a look ☐ **Nearly there** ☐ **Nailed it** ☐

moche	ugly
mûr(e)	mature
optimiste	optimistic

Common adjectives: opinions

amusant(e)	fun, amusing
bruyant(e)	noisy
cher/-ère	expensive
chouette	great (fantastic)
démodé(e)	old fashioned
dur(e)	hard
effrayant(e)	frightening

facile	easy, simple
fantastique	fantastic
fatigant(e)	tiring
favori(te)	favourite
formidable	great (marvellous)
génial(e)	great (fantastic)
idéal(e)	ideal
incroyable	unbelievable
injuste	unfair
inutile	useless
juste	fair

Had a look ☐   Nearly there ☐   Nailed it ☐

magnifique	magnificent
malsain(e)	unhealthy
merveilleux/-euse	marvellous
nécessaire	necessary
négatif/-ve	negative
parfait(e)	perfect
passionnant(e)	exciting
positif/-ve	positive
pratique	practical
préféré(e)	favourite
raisonnable	reasonable
ridicule	ridiculous
sain(e)	healthy (food/way of life)
sensationnel(le)	sensational
sensass	sensational
super	great (fantastic)
simple	easy, simple
superbe	superb
utile	useful
valable	valid
vrai(e)	true

Had a look ☐   Nearly there ☐   Nailed it ☐

Other common adjectives

à la mode	fashionable
ancien(ne)	former, old
autre	other
chaud(e)	hot
court(e)	short
d'une grande valeur	valuable
dernier/-ière	last
étroit(e)	thin, narrow
fermé à clef	locked
grand(e)	large, big
gratuit(e)	free (at no cost)
grave	serious
gros(se)	large, big

haut	high, tall (building)
léger/-ère	light
libre	free (unoccupied, available)
long(ue)	long
lourd(e)	heavy

Had a look ☐   Nearly there ☐   Nailed it ☐

même	same
moderne	modern
mouillé(e)	wet
mûr(e)	ripe
neuf/-ve	new (brand new)
nombreux/-euse	numerous
normal(e)	normal
nouveau/nouvel/nouvelle	new
ouvert(e)	open

Had a look ☐   Nearly there ☐   Nailed it ☐

pareil(le)	alike, the same
plein(e)	full
pourri(e)	rotten
prêt(e)	ready
prochain(e)	next
propre	own
rangé(e)	tidy
rapide	fast
récent(e)	recent
reconnu(e)	recognised, well known
réel(le)	real
silencieux/-ieuse	silent
situé(e)	situated
tranquille	peaceful, quiet, calm
type	typical

Had a look ☐   Nearly there ☐   Nailed it ☐

Comparisons/Superlatives

plus/moins	more/less
plus que/moins que	more than/less than
bon/meilleur/le meilleur	good/better/best
mauvais/pire/le pire	bad/worse/worst
bien/mieux/le mieux	well/better/best
mal/plus mal/le plus mal	badly/worse/worst
beaucoup/plus/le plus	a lot, lots/more/the most
peu/moins/le moins	few, little/less/the least

Had a look ☐   Nearly there ☐   Nailed it ☐

Common adverbs

à peine	hardly
assez	fairly, quite

aussi	too, as well	au fond	in the background, at the back
trop	too	au fond de	at the back of, at the bottom of
bien	well	au lieu de	instead of
bientôt	soon	au milieu (de)	in the middle (of)
bon marché	cheap(ly)	au premier plan	in the foreground
d'habitude	usually	au-dessus de	above
debout	standing	autour de	around
déjà	already	avant	before
encore	again	avec	with
ensemble	together	chez	at (someone's house)
fort	loud(ly)	contre	against
(mal)heureusement	(un)fortunately	dans	in (inside)
ici	here	de	from
immédiatement	immediately	dehors	outside
jamais	never		
là	there		
là-bas	over there		
là-haut	up there		
longtemps	(for) a long time		

Had a look ☐ **Nearly there** ☐ **Nailed it** ☐

		depuis	since, for
		derrière	behind
		devant	in front of, in the front
normalement	usually	en	in, within (time)
nulle part	nowhere	en dehors de	outside (of)
partout	everywhere	en face de	opposite
pas encore	not yet	en haut	above
peut-être	perhaps	en-dessous	under/underneath
plutôt	rather	entre	between
presque	almost	jusqu'à	until
quelque part	somewhere	loin de	far from
quelquefois	sometimes	malgré	despite, in spite of
rarement	rarely	nulle part	nowhere
récemment	recently	par	through
souvent	often	parmi	among(st)
surtout	especially	pour	for, in order to
toujours	always, still	près (de)	near (to)
tout de suite	straight away, immediately	sans	without
très	very	selon	according to
vite	quickly	sous	under/underneath
vraiment	really	sur	on (on top of)
		vers	towards

Had a look ☐ **Nearly there** ☐ **Nailed it** ☐

Prepositions

à	at, to
à côté de	next to
à partir de	from
à travers	across
après	after
au bord de	at the side/edge of
au bout de	at the end of

Connectives

à cause de	because of
à part	apart from
ainsi	so, therefore
alors	so, therefore, then
aussi	also
car	because
cependant	however

c'est-à-dire	*that is to say, i.e.*	vingt-trois	*23*
comme	*as, like*	vingt-quatre	*24*
d'un côté/de l'autre côté	*on the one hand/on the other hand*	vingt-cinq	*25*
		vingt-six	*26*
donc	*so, therefore*	vingt-sept	*27*

Had a look ☐ **Nearly there** ☐ **Nailed it** ☐

		vingt-huit	*28*
		vingt-neuf	*29*
		trente	*30*
ensuite	*next*	trente et un	*31*
évidemment	*obviously*	trente-deux, etc.	*32, etc.*
mais	*but*	quarante	*40*
même si	*even if*	cinquante	*50*
ou	*or*	soixante	*60*
par contre	*on the other hand*		
par exemple	*for example*		

Had a look ☐ **Nearly there** ☐ **Nailed it** ☐

pendant que	*while*		
pourtant	*however*	soixante-dix	*70*
puis	*then*	soixante et onze	*71*
puisque	*seeing that, since*	soixante-douze	*72*
quand	*when*	soixante-treize	*73*
sans doute	*undoubtedly, without doubt, probably*	soixante-quatorze	*74*
		soixante-quinze	*75*
si	*if*	soixante-seize	*76*
y compris	*including*	soixante-dix-sept	*77*

Had a look ☐ **Nearly there** ☐ **Nailed it** ☐

		soixante-dix-huit	*78*
		soixante-dix-neuf	*79*

Had a look ☐ **Nearly there** ☐ **Nailed it** ☐

Numbers

un(e)	*1*		
deux	*2*	quatre-vingts	*80*
trois	*3*	quatre-vingt-un	*81*
quatre	*4*	quatre-vingt-deux, etc.	*82, etc.*
cinq	*5*	quatre-vingt-dix	*90*
six	*6*	quatre-vingt-onze	*91*
sept	*7*	quatre-vingt-douze, etc.	*92, etc.*
huit	*8*		

Had a look ☐ **Nearly there** ☐ **Nailed it** ☐

neuf	*9*		
dix	*10*	cent (m)	*100*
onze	*11*	cent un(e)	*101*
douze	*12*	cent vingt	*120*
treize	*13*	deux cents	*200*
quatorze	*14*	mille (m)	*1000*
quinze	*15*	mille cent	*1100*
seize	*16*	deux mille	*2000*
dix-sept	*17*	un million (m)	*1,000,000*
dix-huit	*18*	deux millions (m)	*2,000,000*
dix-neuf	*19*	premier/-ière	*first*

Had a look ☐ **Nearly there** ☐ **Nailed it** ☐

		deuxième	*second*
vingt	*20*	onzième	*eleventh*
vingt et un	*21*	vingt-et-unième	*twenty first*
vingt-deux	*22*		

Had a look ☐ **Nearly there** ☐ **Nailed it** ☐

High-frequency words

Opinions

à mon avis	*in my opinion*
absolument	*absolutely*
bien entendu	*of course*
bien sûr	*of course*
ça dépend	*that depends*
ça m'énerve	*it gets on my nerves*
ça me fait rire	*it makes me laugh*
ça me plaît	*I like it*
ça m'est égal	*it's all the same to me*
ça ne me dit rien	*it means nothing to me, I don't fancy that, I don't feel like it*
ça suffit	*that's enough*
ça ne fait rien	*it doesn't matter*
ce n'est pas la peine	*it's not worth it*
d'accord	*OK (in agreement)*
j'en ai assez/marre	*I've had enough*
personnellement	*personally*

Had a look ☐ **Nearly there** ☐ **Nailed it** ☐

Other useful expressions

à bientôt	*see you soon*
à demain/vendredi	*see you tomorrow/on Friday*
bonne chance	*good luck*
bon courage	*good luck*
Ça s'écrit comment?	*How do you spell that?*
ça va	*I'm fine, it's OK*
comme çi, comme ça	*so-so*
désolé(e)	*sorry*
défense de	*you are not allowed to*
dommage	*what a shame*
excuse-/excusez-moi	*(I'm) sorry (informal/formal)*
il est interdit de	*you are not allowed to*

Had a look ☐ **Nearly there** ☐ **Nailed it** ☐

il faut	*you must/one must*
il y a	*there is/are*
je ne comprends pas	*I don't understand*
je ne sais pas	*I don't know*
merci (bien)	*thank you (very much)*
Qu'est-ce que cela veut dire?	*What does that mean?*
avec plaisir	*with pleasure*
tant mieux	*all/so much the better*
tant pis	*too bad*
voici	*here is/are*
voilà	*there is/are (i.e. over there)*
volontiers	*with pleasure*

Had a look ☐ **Nearly there** ☐ **Nailed it** ☐

Other useful little words

ça/cela	*that*
le chiffre	*figure (number)*
la chose	*thing*
comme	*as, like*
la façon	*way (manner)*
la fois	*time (occasion)*
le genre	*type (kind of)*
madame	*Mrs, Madam*
mademoiselle	*Miss*
monsieur	*Mr, Sir*
le nombre	*number*
le numéro	*number (phone number)*
par exemple	*for example*
quelqu'un	*someone*
quelque chose	*something*
sauf	*except*
la sorte	*type (kind of)*
tout le monde	*everybody*

Had a look ☐ **Nearly there** ☐ **Nailed it** ☐

Time, frequency and sequencing expressions

à … heure(s)	*at … o'clock*
à … heure(s) et quart	*at quarter past …*
à … heure(s) et demie	*at half past …*
à … heure(s) moins le quart	*at quarter to …*
à la fois	*at the same time*
à l'avenir	*in future, from now on*
à l'heure	*on time*
à temps partiel	*part-time*
l'an (m)	*year*
l'année (f)	*year*
après	*after*
après-demain	*the day after tomorrow*
après-midi	*afternoon*
aujourd'hui	*today*
auparavant	*formerly, in the past*
avant	*before*
avant-hier	*the day before yesterday*
bientôt	*soon*

Had a look ☐ **Nearly there** ☐ **Nailed it** ☐

d'abord	*at first, firstly*
dans le futur	*in the future*
d'habitude	*usually*
de bonne heure	*early*
le début	*start*
demain	*tomorrow*

dernier/dernière	last
de temps en temps	from time to time
déjà	already
de nouveau	again
en attendant	whilst waiting (for), meanwhile
en avance	in advance
en ce moment	at the moment
en retard	late
en train de (faire…)	(to be) doing
en même temps	at the same time
encore une fois	once more, again
enfin	at last, finally
environ	about, approximately

Had a look ☐   **Nearly there** ☐   **Nailed it** ☐

la fin	end
hier	yesterday
il y a	ago
le jour	day
la journée	day
le lendemain	the next day
longtemps	for a long time
maintenant	now
le matin	morning
le mois	month
normalement	normally
la nuit	night
parfois	sometimes
le passé	past
pendant	during
plus tard	later
presque	almost, nearly
prochain	next

Had a look ☐   **Nearly there** ☐   **Nailed it** ☐

quelquefois	sometimes
rarement	rarely
récemment	recently
la semaine	week
seulement	only
le siècle	century
le soir	evening
soudain	suddenly
souvent	often
suivant	following
sur le point de (être)	(to be) about to
tard	late
tôt	early
toujours	always, still
tous les jours	every day

tout à coup	suddenly, all of a sudden
tout de suite	immediately
vite	quickly

Had a look ☐   **Nearly there** ☐   **Nailed it** ☐

Question words

Comment?	How?
Combien (de)?	How much, How many?
Que?	What?
Qu'est-ce qui?	What? (as subject)
Qu'est-ce que?	What? (as object)
Quoi?	What?
De quelle couleur?	What colour?
Comment?	What like?
À quelle heure?	(At) what time?
Quel/Quelle?	What/which?
Quand?	When?
Où?	Where?
Lequel/Laquelle/Lesquels/Lesquelles?	Which one(s)?
Qui?	Who?
Pourquoi?	Why?

Had a look ☐   **Nearly there** ☐   **Nailed it** ☐

Colours

blanc(he)	white
bleu(e)	blue
brun(e)	brown
châtain (invariable)	chestnut brown
clair(e)	light
foncé(e)	dark
gris(e)	grey
jaune	yellow
marron (invariable)	brown, chestnut brown
noir(e)	black
rose	pink
rouge	red
vert(e)	green
violet(te)	violet

Had a look ☐   **Nearly there** ☐   **Nailed it** ☐

Days, months and seasons of the year

lundi	Monday
mardi	Tuesday
mercredi	Wednesday
jeudi	Thursday
vendredi	Friday
samedi	Saturday
dimanche	Sunday

Had a look ☐   **Nearly there** ☐   **Nailed it** ☐

le mois	month
janvier	January
février	February
mars	March
avril	April
mai	May
juin	June
juillet	July
août	August
septembre	September
octobre	October
novembre	November
décembre	December

Had a look ☐ **Nearly there** ☐ **Nailed it** ☐

la saison	season
(en) automne (m)	(in) autumn
(au) printemps (m)	(in) spring
(en) été (m)	(in) summer
(en) hiver (m)	(in) winter

Had a look ☐ **Nearly there** ☐ **Nailed it** ☐

Quantities and measures

assez (de)	enough
beaucoup (de)	a lot (of), many
un centilitre	centilitre
un centimètre	centimetre
demi	half
une gramme	gramme
un kilomètre	kilometre
un mètre	metre
moins (de)	less
more encore (de)	(some)
pas mal (de)	quite a few
(un) peu (de)	a little of, few
plus (de)	more
plusieurs	several
le poids	weight
la quantité	quantity
un quart	quarter
quelques	some
un tiers	third
trop (de)	too much, too many

Had a look ☐ **Nearly there** ☐ **Nailed it** ☐

un kilo (de)	a kilo (of)
un litre (de)	a litre (of)
un morceau (de)	a piece (of)
un paquet (de)	a packet (of)
un peu (de)	a little (of)

un pot (de)	a jar (of)
une boîte (de)	a tin (of), a box (of)
une bouteille (de)	a bottle (of)
une centaine (de)	about a hundred
une douzaine (de)	a dozen
une tranche (de)	a slice (of)
une vingtaine (de)	about twenty

Had a look ☐ **Nearly there** ☐ **Nailed it** ☐

Countries

l'Algérie (f)	Algeria
l'Allemagne (f)	Germany
l'Angleterre (f)	England
l''Autriche (f)	Austria
la Belgique	Belgium
le Canada	Canada
la Chine	China
le Danemark	Denmark
la France	France
la Grande-Bretagne	Great Britain
la Grèce	Greece
la Hollande	Holland

Had a look ☐ **Nearly there** ☐ **Nailed it** ☐

l'Inde (f)	India
l'Irlande (f)	Ireland
l'Italie (f)	Italy
les Pays-Bas (m)	the Netherlands
le Pakistan	Pakistan
la Russie	Russia
l'Écosse (f)	Scotland
le Sénégal	Senegal
l'Espagne (f)	Spain
la Suisse	Switzerland
la Tunisie	Tunisia
la Turquie	Turkey
le Royaume-Uni	United Kingdom
les États-Unis (m)	the United States
le pays de Galles	Wales

Had a look ☐ **Nearly there** ☐ **Nailed it** ☐

Continents

l'Afrique (f)	Africa
l'Asie (f)	Asia
l'Australie (f)	Australia
l'Europe (f)	Europe
l'Amérique du Nord (f)	North America
l'Amérique du Sud (f)	South America

Had a look ☐ **Nearly there** ☐ **Nailed it** ☐

Nationalities

algérien(ne)	*Algerian*
allemand(e)	*German*
américain(e)	*American*
anglais(e)	*English*
autrichien(ne)	*Austrian*
belge	*Belgian*
britannique	*British*
canadien(ne)	*Canadian*
chinois(e)	*Chinese*
corse	*Corsican*
danois(e)	*Danish*
écossais(e)	*Scottish*
espagnol(e)	*Spanish*
européen(ne)	*European*
français(e)	*French*
gallois(e)	*Welsh*
grec(que)	*Greek*
hollandais(e)	*Dutch*

Had a look ☐   **Nearly there** ☐   **Nailed it** ☐

indien(ne)	*Indian*
irlandais(e)	*Irish*
italien(ne)	*Italian*
pakistanais(e)	*Pakistani*
russe	*Russian*
suisse	*Swiss*
tunisien(ne)	*Tunisian*
turque	*Turkish*

Had a look ☐   **Nearly there** ☐   **Nailed it** ☐

Geographical surroundings

à droite	*on/to the right*
à gauche	*on/to the left*
chez	*at the house of*
de chaque côté	*from each side*
de l'autre côté	*from the other side*
en bas	*down(stairs)*
en haut	*up(stairs)*
ici	*here*
là	*there*
là-bas	*over there*

Had a look ☐   **Nearly there** ☐   **Nailed it** ☐

la banlieue	*suburb*
la campagne	*countryside*
le centre-ville	*town centre*
la ville	*town*

Had a look ☐   **Nearly there** ☐   **Nailed it** ☐

loin de	*far from*
nulle part	*nowhere*
par	*by*
partout	*everywhere*
quelque part	*somewhere*
situé(e)	*situated*
tout droit	*straight ahead*
tout près	*very near*
toutes directions	*all directions*

Had a look ☐   **Nearly there** ☐   **Nailed it** ☐

l'est (m)	*east*
l'ouest (m)	*west*
le nord	*north*
le sud	*south*

Had a look ☐   **Nearly there** ☐   **Nailed it** ☐

Materials

l'argent (m)	*silver*
le béton	*concrete*
le bois	*wood*
le cuir	*leather*
le fer	*iron*
la laine	*wool*
l'or (m)	*gold*
la soie	*silk*
le verre	*glass*

Had a look ☐   **Nearly there** ☐   **Nailed it** ☐

Climate

l'averse (f)	*shower*
briller	*to shine*
le brouillard	*fog*
la brume	*mist*
la chaleur	*heat*
le ciel	*sky*
le climat	*climate*
couvert	*overcast*
doux	*mild*
l'éclair (m)	*lightning*
l'éclaircie (f)	*bright spell*
ensoleillé	*sunny*
faire beau	*to be fine (weather)*
faire mauvais	*to be bad (weather)*
geler	*to freeze*
la glace	*ice*
humide	*humid, wet*
la météo	*weather forecast*
mouillé	*wet*

Had a look ☐   **Nearly there** ☐   **Nailed it** ☐

13

neiger	*to snow*
le nuage	*cloud*
nuageux	*cloudy*
l'ombre (f)	*shade, shadow*
l'orage (m)	*storm*
orageux	*stormy*
pleuvoir	*to rain*
la pluie	*rain*
sec	*dry*
la tempête	*storm*
le temps	*weather*
le tonnerre	*thunder*
tremper	*to soak*
le vent	*wind*

Had a look ☐ **Nearly there** ☐ **Nailed it** ☐

Social conventions

à plus tard	*see you later*
à tout à l'heure	*see you later*
allô	*hello (on the telephone)*
amitiés	*best wishes*
amuse-toi/amusez-vous bien!	*enjoy yourself/yourselves!*
au revoir	*goodbye*
au secours	*help!*
bien sûr	*of course*
bon voyage	*have a good journey*
bonjour	*hello, good morning*
bonne journée	*have a good day*
bonne nuit	*goodnight*
bonne soirée	*have a good evening*
bonsoir	*good evening*
de rien	*don't mention it*
Je t'/vous en prie	*It's a pleasure*
non merci	*no thank you*
pardon?	*I beg your pardon? Pardon?*
prière de	*please (request – formal)*
rendez-vous (m)	*meeting, meeting place*
rendez-vous à six heures	*meet you at 6 o'clock*
s'il te plaît/s'il vous plaît	*please (informal)/please (polite)*
salut	*hi*
veuillez	*please (request – formal)*

Had a look ☐ **Nearly there** ☐ **Nailed it** ☐

Words I should know for speaking and writing activities

La famille	*Family members*
les parents (m)	parents
le père	father
la mère	mother
le beau-père	stepfather, father-in-law
la belle-mère	stepmother, mother-in-law
le mari	husband
la femme	wife
les enfants (m)	children
le fils	son
la fille	daughter
le frère	brother
la sœur	sister

Had a look ☐ **Nearly there** ☐ **Nailed it** ☐

le demi-frère	half-brother, stepbrother
la demi-sœur	half-sister, stepsister
le beau-frère	brother-in-law
la belle-sœur	sister-in-law
les grands-parents (m)	grandparents
le grand-père	grandfather
la grand-mère	grandmother
les petits-enfants (m)	grandchildren
le petit-fils	grandson
la petite-fille	granddaughter
l'oncle (m)	uncle
la tante	aunt
le cousin/la cousine	cousin

Had a look ☐ **Nearly there** ☐ **Nailed it** ☐

Les adjectifs de personnalité	*Personality adjectives*
Il/Elle est …	He/She is …
agaçant(e)	annoying
arrogant(e)	arrogant
amusant(e)	amusing, funny
bavard(e)	talkative, chatty
charmant(e)	charming
content(e)	happy
fort(e)	strong
impatient(e)	impatient
impoli(e)	impolite
indépendant(e)	independent
intelligent(e)	intelligent
marrant(e)	funny
méchant(e)	nasty, mean
têtu(e)	stubborn, pig-headed

Had a look ☐ **Nearly there** ☐ **Nailed it** ☐

Ma description physique	*My physical description*
J'ai les cheveux …	I have …
courts/longs	short/long hair
raides/bouclés/frisés	straight/curly hair
noirs/bruns/blonds	black/brown/blond hair
roux/gris/blancs	red/grey/white hair
J'ai les yeux …	I have …
bleus/verts	blue/green eyes
gris/marron	grey/brown eyes
J'ai …	I have …
des lunettes	glasses
des boutons	spots
une moustache	a moustache
une barbe	a beard
Je suis …	I am …
petit(e)/grand(e)	short/tall
de taille moyenne	of average height
mince/gros(se)	thin/fat

Had a look ☐ **Nearly there** ☐ **Nailed it** ☐

En ville	*In town*
la boîte de nuit	night club
le bowling	bowling alley
le café	café
le centre commercial	shopping centre
le cinéma	cinema
les magasins (m)	shops
la patinoire	ice rink
la piscine	swimming pool
la plage	beach
le théâtre	theatre
dans	in
derrière	behind
devant	in front of
entre	between

Had a look ☐ **Nearly there** ☐ **Nailed it** ☐

Quand?	*When?*
aujourd'hui	today
demain	tomorrow
ce/demain matin	this/tomorrow morning
cet/demain après-midi	this/tomorrow afternoon
ce/demain soir	this/tomorrow evening
lundi matin	on Monday morning
samedi soir	on Saturday night

Had a look ☐ **Nearly there** ☐ **Nailed it** ☐

Les amis	*Friends*
l'ami (m)/le copain	(male) friend
l'amie (f)/la copine	(female) friend
le petit ami/le petit copain	boyfriend

M 1

la petite amie/la petite copine	girlfriend
Je retrouve mes amis au parc.	I meet up with my friends in the park.
Je traîne en ville avec mes copines.	I hang out in town with my (female) friends.
Je tchatte en ligne avec ma meilleure copine.	I chat online with my best (female) friend.
Avec mon petit ami, j'écoute de la musique.	I listen to music with my boyfriend.
Je passe chez ma petite copine.	I go to my girlfriend's house.
On rigole bien ensemble.	We have a good laugh together.
On regarde un film ou des clips vidéo.	We watch a film or music videos.
On joue au foot ou au basket ensemble.	We play football or basketball together.
On discute de tout.	We talk about everything.
On mange ensemble au fast-food.	We eat together at a fast-food restaurant.

Had a look ☐ **Nearly there** ☐ **Nailed it** ☐

L'amitié
Friendship

Je pense que …	I think that …
Pour moi, …	For me …
À mon avis, …	In my opinion …
Un(e) bon(ne) ami(e) est …	A good friend is …
compréhensif/-ive	understanding
cool	cool
drôle	funny
fidèle	loyal
généreux/-euse	generous
gentil(le)	kind
honnête	honest
modeste	modest
optimiste	optimistic
patient(e)	patient
sensible	sensitive
sympa	nice

Had a look ☐ **Nearly there** ☐ **Nailed it** ☐

Un(e) bon(ne) ami(e) …	A good friend …
écoute mes problèmes/ mes secrets	listens to my problems/ my secrets
discute de tout avec moi	talks about everything with me
aide tout le monde	helps everyone
accepte mes imperfections	accepts my faults
respecte mes opinions	respects my opinions
a les mêmes centres d'intérêt que moi	has the same interests as me
a le sens de l'humour	has a sense of humour

Had a look ☐ **Nearly there** ☐ **Nailed it** ☐

Les rapports de famille
Family relationships

Je m'entends bien avec …	I get on well with …
Je me dispute avec …	I argue with …
Je me chamaille avec …	I bicker with …
Je m'amuse avec …	I have fun with …
Je m'occupe de …	I look after …
le frère aîné/cadet	older/younger brother
la sœur aînée/cadette	older/younger sister
Il/Elle est/a l'air/ semble …	He/She is/looks/ seems …
dynamique	lively
égoïste	selfish
jaloux/-ouse	jealous
sévère	strict
timide	shy
travailleur/-euse	hard-working

Had a look ☐ **Nearly there** ☐ **Nailed it** ☐

On va sortir
Going out

Je vais …	I am going …
aller à un match	to go to a match
aller au bowling	to go to the bowling alley
aller au cinéma	to go to the cinema
aller à la piscine	to go to the swimming pool
voir un spectacle	to see a show
faire du patin à glace	to go ice-skating
faire du skate	to go skateboarding
faire les magasins	to go shopping
jouer à des jeux vidéo	to play video games
Tu veux venir?	Do you want to come?

Had a look ☐ **Nearly there** ☐ **Nailed it** ☐

Les questions
Questions

Quand?	When?
Avec qui?	With who/whom?
On y va comment?	How are we getting there?
On se retrouve où?	Where shall we meet?
On se retrouve à quelle heure?	At what time shall we meet?

Had a look ☐ **Nearly there** ☐ **Nailed it** ☐

Une sortie
An outing

J'ai contacté un copain/ une copine.	I contacted a friend.
J'ai quitté la maison.	I left the house.
J'ai raté le bus.	I missed the bus.
Je suis allé(e) en ville.	I went into town.
J'ai écouté de la musique.	I listened to music.
J'ai retrouvé mon copain/ma copine.	I met up with my friend.

J'ai discuté avec mon copain/ma copine.	*I talked to my friend.*
J'ai mangé un sandwich.	*I ate a sandwich.*
J'ai acheté des vêtements.	*I bought some clothes.*
C'était super.	*It was great.*
J'ai passé une très bonne journée.	*I had a very good day.*

Had a look ☐ **Nearly there** ☐ **Nailed it** ☐

La personne que j'admire
The person I admire

Comment s'appelle la personne que tu admires?	*What is the name of the person you admire?*
Mon héros s'appelle …	*My hero is called …*
Mon héroïne s'appelle …	*My heroine is called …*
Mon modèle s'appelle …	*My role model is called …*
C'est qui?	*Who is he/she?*
C'est un pilote de Formule 1.	*He is a Formula 1 driver.*
C'est un scientifique.	*He is a scientist.*
C'est une actrice.	*She is an actress.*
C'est une créatrice de mode.	*She is a fashion designer.*
Fais-moi sa description physique.	*Describe for me what he/she looks like.*

Had a look ☐ **Nearly there** ☐ **Nailed it** ☐

Il/Elle est …	*He/She is …*
petit(e)/gros(se), etc.	*small/fat, etc.*
Il/Elle a les cheveux bruns, etc.	*He/She has brown hair, etc.*
Quelle est sa personnalité?	*What is his/her personality?*
Il/Elle est …	*He/She is …*
travailleur/-euse/ créatif/-ive, etc.	*hard-working/creative, etc.*
Pourquoi est-ce que tu admires cette personne?	*Why do you admire this person?*
J'admire (Stromae/ Malala, etc.) car il/elle …	*I admire (Stromae/Malala, etc.) because he/she …*
a travaillé très dur	*worked/has worked very hard*
a joué dans beaucoup de films	*acted/has acted in lots of films*
a gagné beaucoup de courses	*won/has won lots of races*
a donné de l'argent à de bonnes œuvres	*gave/has given money to good causes*
a lutté contre ses problèmes	*fought/has fought his/ her problems*
J'aimerais être comme lui/elle.	*I would like to be like him/her.*

Had a look ☐ **Nearly there** ☐ **Nailed it** ☐

Extra words I should know for reading and listening activities

Moi | Me
Je suis … — I am …
Je m'appelle …* — I am called …
Je joue le rôle de … — I play the part of …

Had a look ☐ Nearly there ☐ Nailed it ☐

La personne que j'admire | The person that I admire
Il/elle a sauvé …** — he/she saved …
Il/elle a aidé …** — he/she helped …
ses vêtements — his/her clothes
ses romans — his/her novels
ses études — his/her studies
son exécution — his/her execution
sa créativité — his/her creativity
sa détermination — his/her determination
un enfant adopté — an adopted child
un(e) auteur(e) — an author

Had a look ☐ Nearly there ☐ Nailed it ☐

un(e) professeur(e) — a teacher
un exemple — an example
un soldat — a soldier
un(e) aviateur/-trice — an aviator
une armée — an army
un camp — a camp
une vie — a life
une université — a university
une maison — a house
une mode — a fashion

Had a look ☐ Nearly there ☐ Nailed it ☐

Comment est ton héros/héroïne? | What is your hero/heroine like?
Il/elle est/était … — He/she is/was …
courageux/-euse — brave
de nationalité (pakistanaise) — of (Pakistani) nationality
jeune — young
fort(e) — strong
francophone — French-speaking
mort(e) — dead
vrai(e) — real
algérien(ne) — Algerian

Had a look ☐ Nearly there ☐ Nailed it ☐

Une visite chez … | A visit to …'s house
On est invité(e)s à (manger) … — We were invited to (eat) …
On a pris le train tôt/tard. — We got the train early/late.
le matin — in the morning
le soir — in the evening

Had a look ☐ Nearly there ☐ Nailed it ☐

*Some verbs in French have three parts to them. Without the third part known as the reflexive pronoun, the verb changes its meaning, for example:

Je m'appelle … — I am called …
J'appelle le chien. — I call the dog.
Elle se lève. — She gets up.
Elle lève la chaise. — She lifts up the chair.

**Past tense actions often end in -é, for example: Il/elle a aidé (he/she helped). Without the é, the meaning of the word changes and its sound changes too.

When you read a word with é, or hear this sound, work out the context to find the meaning.

Words I should know for speaking and writing activities

Les passe-temps — *Hobbies*
Je joue … — *I play …*
au badminton — *badminton*
au basket — *basketball*
au billard — *snooker*
au foot — *football*
au golf — *golf*
au hockey — *hockey*
au rugby — *rugby*
au tennis — *tennis*
au volley — *volleyball*
à la pétanque — *French bowls*
aux cartes (f) — *cards*
aux échecs (m) — *chess*
du piano — *the piano*
du saxophone — *the saxophone*
du violon — *the violin*
de la batterie — *the drums*
de la guitare — *the guitar*
de l'accordéon (m) — *the accordion*
de l'harmonica (m) — *the harmonica*

Had a look ☐ **Nearly there** ☐ **Nailed it** ☐

Les expressions de fréquence — *Frequency expressions*
tous les jours — *every day*
tous les soirs — *every evening*
tous les samedis — *every Saturday*
une fois par semaine — *once a week*
deux fois par semaine — *twice a week*
souvent — *often*
de temps en temps — *from time to time*
rarement — *rarely*

Had a look ☐ **Nearly there** ☐ **Nailed it** ☐

Les opinions — *Opinions*
Je trouve ça … — *I find that …*
cool/génial — *cool/great*
passionnant/super — *exciting/super*
ennuyeux/nul — *boring/rubbish*
stupide — *stupid*

Had a look ☐ **Nearly there** ☐ **Nailed it** ☐

J'aime et je n'aime pas … — *I like and I don't like …*
Ma passion, c'est … — *My passion is …*
le cinéma/le sport/la musique — *the cinema/sport/music*
J'aime/J'adore/Je préfère … — *I like/love/prefer …*
Je n'aime pas/Je déteste … — *I don't like/hate …*

le foot/jouer au foot — *football/playing football*
la lecture/lire — *reading*
la photographie/prendre des photos — *photography/taking photos*

Had a look ☐ **Nearly there** ☐ **Nailed it** ☐

Les films — *Films*
une comédie — *a comedy*
un western — *a Western*
un film fantastique — *a fantasy film*
un film d'action — *an action film*
un film d'arts martiaux — *a martial arts film*
un film d'aventure — *an adventure film*
un film d'horreur — *a horror film*
un film de gangsters — *a gangster film*
un film de science-fiction — *a science fiction film*

Had a look ☐ **Nearly there** ☐ **Nailed it** ☐

Acheter des billets — *Buying tickets*
Qu'est-ce qu'il y a au cinéma? — *What's on at the cinema?*
La séance commence à quelle heure? — *At what time does the screening start?*
Je peux vous aider? — *Can I help you?*
Je voudrais deux billets pour … — *I would like two tickets for …*
Pour quelle séance? — *For which screening?*
Pour la séance de 19 heures. — *For the screening at 7 p.m.*
Ça coûte combien? — *How much does it cost?*
Le tarif réduit, c'est 14 euros la place. — *The reduced price is 14 euros per seat.*

Had a look ☐ **Nearly there** ☐ **Nailed it** ☐

Le sport — *Sport*
Je fais … — *I …*
du footing — *go jogging*
du trampoline — *do trampolining*
du vélo — *go cycling*
de la boxe — *do boxing*
de la danse — *go dancing*
de la natation — *go swimming*
de l'équitation (f) — *go horse-riding*
de l'escalade (f) — *go climbing*
de l'escrime (f) — *do fencing*
des randonnées (f) — *go hiking*
Je fais ça depuis … — *I have been doing that for …*
six mois — *six months*
deux ans — *two years*

Had a look ☐ **Nearly there** ☐ **Nailed it** ☐

Parler de sport / Talking about sport

Parler de sport	Talking about sport
Je préfère les sports individuels.	I prefer individual sports.
Je préfère les sports d'équipe.	I prefer team sports.
Je trouve ça rigolo/facile/rapide	I find it/that fun/easy/fast
Ça me fait du bien.	It does me good.
Ça me détend.	It relaxes me.
Ça booste le moral.	It boosts my/your mood.
C'est bon pour le corps et le mental.	It's good for the body and the mind.
Quand je fais ça, …	When I do/I'm doing it, …
je respire	I breathe
j'oublie mes soucis	I forget my worries

Had a look ☐ **Nearly there** ☐ **Nailed it** ☐

Sur mon téléphone portable/ma tablette, … / On my phone/tablet, …

Sur mon téléphone portable/ma tablette, …	On my phone/tablet, …
je crée des playlists	I create playlists
je télécharge de la musique	I download music
je regarde des clips vidéo	I watch music videos
je joue à des jeux	I play games
je fais des recherches pour mes devoirs	I do research for my homework
je fais des achats	I buy things
j'écris des messages	I write messages
j'écris des articles pour mon blog	I write posts for my blog
je lis mes e-mails	I read my emails
je vais sur des réseaux sociaux	I go onto social media sites
je prends des photos	I take photos
je mets mes photos sur Instagram ou Snapchat	I put my photos on Instagram or Snapchat
À mon avis, c'est …	In my opinion, it's …
génial	great
très pratique	very practical
indispensable	essential

Had a look ☐ **Nearly there** ☐ **Nailed it** ☐

Internet / The internet

Internet	The internet
Il est facile de/d' …	It is easy to …
Il est possible de/d' …	It is possible to …
rester en contact avec ses amis	stay in contact with your friends
faire des recherches pour ses devoirs	do research for your homework
utiliser un dico en ligne	use an online dictionary
partager des photos	share photos
Il est dangereux de …	It is dangerous to …
partager ses détails personnels	share your personal details
passer trop de temps sur Internet	spend too much time on the internet
tchatter en ligne avec des inconnus	chat to strangers online
Il est important de …	It is important to …
faire du sport	do some sport
passer du temps avec sa famille	spend some time with your family
retrouver ses amis en vrai	meet up with your friends in real life

Had a look ☐ **Nearly there** ☐ **Nailed it** ☐

La lecture / Reading

La lecture	Reading
J'apprécie beaucoup les …	I really appreciate/like …
Je préfère les …	I prefer …
J'adore les …	I love …
J'ai une passion pour les …	I'm passionate about …
Je n'aime pas les …	I don't like …
J'ai horreur des …	I hate …
romans fantastiques	fantasy novels
romans policiers	detective novels
romans d'amour	romance novels
livres d'épouvante	horror books
BD	comic books, graphic novels
mangas	mangas
J'aime les illustrations/l'humour.	I like the illustrations/humour.
Je ne lis pas sur une tablette.	I don't read on a tablet.
Je préfère tenir un livre traditionnel dans mes mains.	I prefer holding a traditional book in my hands.
Je ne lis plus de livres traditionnels.	I no longer read traditional books.
Je lis beaucoup en ligne.	I read a lot online.

Had a look ☐ **Nearly there** ☐ **Nailed it** ☐

La musique / Music

La musique	Music
J'aime … /Je n'aime pas …	I like … /I don't like …
le jazz	jazz
le rap	rap
le reggae	reggae
le rock	rock
la musique classique	classical music
la musique pop	pop music
J'écoute ma musique …	I listen to my music …
sur mon téléphone portable avec mes écouteurs.	on my phone with my earphones.
sur mon ordi	on my computer
sur une tablette	on a tablet
Je regarde des clips vidéo pour écouter ma musique.	I watch music videos to listen to my music.

Mon chanteur préféré/ ma chanteuse préférée, c'est … car …	My favourite singer is … because …
j'aime ses paroles	I like his/her lyrics
j'aime ses mélodies	I like his/her tunes
sa musique me donne envie de danser	his/her music makes me want to dance
sa musique me donne envie de chanter	his/her music makes me want to sing

Had a look ☐   Nearly there ☐   Nailed it ☐

Les émissions de télé — TV programmes

J'aime/Je n'aime pas …	I like/I don't like …
les documentaires (m)	documentaries
les jeux télévisés (m)	game shows
les magazines culturels (m)	magazine programmes
les séries (f)	series
les émissions de sport (f)	sports programmes
les émissions de musique (f)	music programmes
les émissions de télé-réalité (f)	reality TV programmes
les actualités (f)	the news
parce qu'ils/elles sont …	because they are/it is …
amusant(e)s	funny
divertissant(e)s	entertaining
intéressant(e)s	interesting
passionnant(e)s	exciting
éducatifs/-ives	educational
ennuyeux/-euses	boring
(trop) sérieux/-euses	(too) serious
originaux/-ales	original

Had a look ☐   Nearly there ☐   Nailed it ☐

Mon émission préférée s'appelle …	My favourite programme is called …
C'est un jeu télévisé.	It's a game show.
C'est une série.	It's a drama series.
J'aime bien l'animateur/-rice.	I like the presenter.
Les acteurs sont très doués.	The actors are very talented.
Le scénario est passionnant.	The plot is exciting.
J'apprends beaucoup.	I learn a lot.
Je ne rate jamais cette émission!	I never miss this programme!

Had a look ☐   Nearly there ☐   Nailed it ☐

Une soirée entre amis — An evening with friends

Je suis allé(e) au cinéma.	I went to the cinema.
Je suis sorti(e) avec …	I went out with …
On est allé(e)s à un concert.	We went to a concert.
On a vu un film.	We saw a film.
On est allé(e)s en ville.	We went into town.
On a fait du patin à glace.	We went ice skating.
J'ai pris beaucoup de photos.	I took lots of photos.
J'ai mis les photos sur Instagram.	I put the photos on Instagram.
On est allé(e)s au restaurant.	We went to a restaurant.
J'ai bu un coca.	I drank a cola.
C'était …	It was …
génial	great
lamentable	pathetic
amusant	fun, funny
délicieux	delicious

Had a look ☐   Nearly there ☐   Nailed it ☐

M 2

21

M 2

Extra words I should know for reading and listening activities

Tu es sportif/ sportive?   *Are you sporty?*

le marathon de (Paris)	*the (Paris) marathon*
les sports rapides (m)	*quick sports*
mon équipe (f)	*my team*
ensemble	*together*

Had a look ☐   **Nearly there** ☐   **Nailed it** ☐

Ma vie d'internaute   *My online life*

le blog*	*blog*
le dico** en ligne	*online dictionary*
le portable	*laptop*
la tablette*	*tablet*
l'ordi** (m)	*computer*
les réseaux sociaux (m)	*social networks*
les écouteurs (m)	*headphones*
apprendre beaucoup de choses	*to learn a lot of things*
partager des détails personnels avec des inconnus	*to share your personal details with strangers*
faire des achats	*to do shopping*
jouer à des jeux	*to play games*
la photographie	*photography*

Had a look ☐   **Nearly there** ☐   **Nailed it** ☐

Je (ne) lis (pas) ...	*I (don't) read ...*
Je trouve ...	*I find ...*
Je préfère ...	*I prefer ...*
Je pense ...	*I think ...*
Je regarde ...	*I watch ...*
Je peux ...	*I can ...*
J'adore ...	*I love ...*
J'aime (bien) ...	*I (really) like ...*
J'apprécie ...	*I appreciate ...*
J'écoute ...	*I listen ...*

Had a look ☐   **Nearly there** ☐   **Nailed it** ☐

⭐ **Remember that you can abbreviate words in French too, for example: *ordi* (*ordinateur*), *dico* (*dictionnaire*). So, if you encounter a word that you don't recognise, think about whether it is a shorter version of a word that you already know. The context that the word is in will help you to do this.

⭐ *Lots of new technology-related words are the same in French as in English, for example: *le blog, la tablette*.

Words I should know for speaking and writing activities

La nourriture et les boissons / *Food and drink*

du beurre	*butter*
du fromage	*cheese*
du lait	*milk*
du pain	*bread*
du poisson	*fish*
du poulet	*chicken*
du yaourt	*yoghurt*
de la confiture	*jam*
de la glace	*ice cream*
de la viande	*meat*
de l'eau (f)	*water*
des bananes (f)	*bananas*
des fraises (f)	*strawberries*
des œufs (m)	*eggs*
des pêches (f)	*peaches*
des poires (f)	*pears*
des pommes (f)	*apples*
des pommes de terre (f)	*potatoes*

Had a look ☐ **Nearly there** ☐ **Nailed it** ☐

Les repas / *Meals*

Qu'est-ce que tu prends pour le petit-déjeuner?	*What do you have for breakfast?*
Qu'est-ce que tu manges à midi?	*What do you eat at lunchtime?*
Qu'est-ce que tu manges comme casse-croûte?	*What do you have as a snack?*
Qu'est-ce que tu manges, le soir?	*What do you eat in the evening?*
Qu'est-ce que tu bois?	*What do you drink?*
Pour le petit-déjeuner, …	*For breakfast, …*
À midi, …	*At lunchtime, …*
Comme casse-croûte, …	*As a snack, …*
Le soir, …	*In the evening, …*
Comme dessert, …	*For dessert, …*
Je prends/Je mange …	*I have/I eat …*
des céréales (f)	*cereal*
du pain grillé	*toast*
un sandwich	*a sandwich*
des chips (f)	*crisps*
des biscuits (m)	*biscuits*
des pâtes (f)	*pasta*
de la salade	*salad*
de la glace au chocolat	*chocolate ice cream*
Je bois du jus d'orange.	*I drink orange juice.*

Had a look ☐ **Nearly there** ☐ **Nailed it** ☐

Les quantités / *Quantities*

un kilo de …	*a kilo of …*
deux cent cinquante grammes de …	*250 grams of …*

un litre de …	*a litre of …*
un paquet de …	*a packet of …*
un pot de …	*a jar/pot of …*
une boîte de …	*a tin/can of …*
une bouteille de …	*a bottle of …*
quatre tranches de …	*four slices of …*

Had a look ☐ **Nearly there** ☐ **Nailed it** ☐

Les vêtements / *Clothes*

Je porte …	*I wear/am wearing …*
un blouson	*a jacket*
un chapeau	*a hat*
un costume	*a suit*
un imperméable	*a raincoat*
un jean (moulant)	*(a pair of) (skinny) jeans*
un manteau	*a coat*
un pantalon	*(a pair of) trousers*
un polo	*a polo shirt*
un pull	*a jumper*
un sac à main	*a handbag*
un short	*(a pair of) shorts*
un sweat à capuche	*a hoody*
un tee-shirt	*a T-shirt*
une casquette	*a cap*
une ceinture	*a belt*

Had a look ☐ **Nearly there** ☐ **Nailed it** ☐

une chemise	*a shirt*
une écharpe	*a scarf*
une mini-jupe	*a miniskirt*
une montre	*a watch*
une robe	*a dress*
une veste	*a jacket*
des baskets (de marque) (f)	*(designer) trainers*
des boucles d'oreille (f)	*earrings*
des bottes (f)	*boots*
des chaussettes (f)	*socks*
des chaussures (f)	*shoes*
des gants (m)	*gloves*
des lunettes de soleil (f)	*sunglasses*
en laine	*woollen*
en cuir	*leather*
rayé(e)(s)	*striped*

Had a look ☐ **Nearly there** ☐ **Nailed it** ☐

Les couleurs / *Colours*

blanc(he)(s)	*white*
bleu(e)(s)	*blue*
gris(e)(s)	*grey*
jaune(s)	*yellow*
marron	*brown*

M 3

mauve(s)	*purple*
noir(e)(s)	*black*
orange	*orange*
rose(s)	*pink*
rouge(s)	*red*
vert(e)(s)	*green*
clair	*light*
foncé	*dark*
multicolore(s)	*multi-coloured*

Had a look ☐ **Nearly there** ☐ **Nailed it** ☐

La vie quotidienne / *Daily life*

J'ai cours tous les jours sauf …	*I have lessons every day except …*
Les jours d'école, …	*On school days …*
je dois me lever tôt	*I have to get up early*
je dois quitter la maison à (7h30)	*I have to leave the house at (7:30 a.m.)*
Le soir, …	*In the evening, …*
je dois faire mes devoirs	*I have to do my homework*
je dois aider ma mère	*I have to help my mother*
je peux regarder un peu la télé	*I can watch a bit of TV*
Le samedi, …	*On Saturdays, …*
Le dimanche, …	*On Sundays, …*
je peux rester au lit	*I can stay in bed*
je peux retrouver mes copains/copines en ville	*I can meet up with my friends in town*
je dois ranger ma chambre	*I have to tidy my room*
je peux écouter de la musique	*I can listen to music*

Had a look ☐ **Nearly there** ☐ **Nailed it** ☐

Au magasin de vêtements / *In the clothes shop*

la taille	*size*
la pointure	*shoe size*
les cabines d'essayage (f)	*changing rooms*
une taille moyenne	*medium size*
Il y a un trou.	*There's a hole (in it).*
Il y a une tache.	*There's a stain (on it).*
Il/Elle est … /Ils/Elles sont …	*It is … /They are …*
trop petit(e)(s)	*too small*
trop grand(e)(s)	*too big*
cassé(e)(s)	*broken*
Il/Elle ne marche pas.	*It is not working/ doesn't work.*
Je voudrais …	*I would like …*
échanger (la jupe/le pantalon, etc.)	*to exchange (the skirt/ trousers, etc.)*
un remboursement	*a refund*

Had a look ☐ **Nearly there** ☐ **Nailed it** ☐

Faire les magasins ou faire du shopping en ligne? / *Go to the shops or shop online?*

Je préfère …	*I prefer …*
faire les magasins	*to go to the shops*
faire mes achats en ligne	*to make my purchases online*
parce que/qu' …	*because …*
c'est mieux d'essayer les vêtements dans un magasin	*it's better to try clothes on in a shop*
je peux demander l'opinion de mes ami(e)s	*I can ask my friends' opinion*
il y a trop de monde dans les magasins	*there are too many people in the shops*
on peut trouver des vêtements moins chers	*you can find cheaper clothes*
c'est plus facile/plus rapide	*it's easier/faster*

Had a look ☐ **Nearly there** ☐ **Nailed it** ☐

Les fêtes / *Festivals*

Noël	*Christmas*
la veille de Noël	*Christmas Eve*
Pâques	*Easter*
Divali	*Diwali*
Hanoukka	*Hanukkah*
Aïd-el-Fitr	*Eid al-Fitr*
le 6 janvier/la fête des Rois	*Epiphany*
le premier avril	*April Fool's Day*
la Chandeleur	*Candlemas*
le Nouvel An	*New Year*
la Saint-Sylvestre	*New Year's Eve*
la Saint-Valentin	*Valentine's Day*
la fête des Mères	*Mother's Day*
le 14 juillet/la fête nationale française	*Bastille Day, 14 July*
On est chrétiens.	*We are Christian.*
On est juifs.	*We are Jewish.*
On est musulmans.	*We are Muslim.*

Had a look ☐ **Nearly there** ☐ **Nailed it** ☐

Chez moi/nous …	*At my/our house …*
on fête (Noël/Divali, etc.)	*we celebrate (Christmas/ Diwali, etc.)*
on boit du champagne	*we drink champagne*
on décore le sapin de Noël	*we decorate the Christmas tree*
on s'offre des cadeaux	*we give each other presents*
on ouvre les cadeaux	*we open the presents*
on chante des chants traditionnels	*we sing traditional songs*
on allume des bougies	*we light candles*

on cherche des œufs dans le jardin	we look for eggs in the garden
On prépare/mange …	We prepare/eat …
de la dinde rôtie	roast turkey
des légumes (m)	vegetables
une bûche de Noël au chocolat	a chocolate Yule log
des crêpes (f)	crêpes
une galette des Rois	tart eaten for Epiphany
toutes sortes de bonnes choses	all sorts of good things
des choses sucrées	sweet things

Had a look ☐ **Nearly there** ☐ **Nailed it** ☐

Un repas spécial — *A special meal*

Je vais/On va apporter …	I am/We are going to bring …
du jambon	ham
du pâté	pâté
du saucisson	salami
des baguettes (f)	baguettes
des biftecks (m)	steaks
des saucisses (f)	sausages
des salades composées (f)	mixed salads
une salade de riz	a rice salad
du concombre	cucumber
une laitue	a lettuce
des tomates (f)	tomatoes
des oignons (m)	onions
des poivrons (m)	peppers
des champignons (m)	mushrooms
des abricots (m)	apricots
des framboises (f)	raspberries
du raisin	grapes
des mini-gâteaux (m)	mini-cakes
une tarte aux fruits	a fruit tart

Had a look ☐ **Nearly there** ☐ **Nailed it** ☐

Les magasins — *Shops*

le marché	market
le supermarché	supermarket
la boucherie	butcher's
la boulangerie	bakery, baker's
la charcuterie	pork butcher's, delicatessen
la pâtisserie	cake shop, pastry shop
l'épicerie (f)	greengrocer's

Had a look ☐ **Nearly there** ☐ **Nailed it** ☐

Fêter le 14 juillet — *Celebrating Bastille Day*

On va aller au bal.	We're going to go to the dance.
On va regarder le feu d'artifice.	We're going to watch the fireworks.
On va s'amuser.	We're going to have fun.
On va inviter …	We're going to invite …

Had a look ☐ **Nearly there** ☐ **Nailed it** ☐

Félicitations! — *Congratulations!*

l'anniversaire (m)	birthday
le mariage	wedding, marriage
la fête	party
C'était mon anniversaire.	It was my birthday.
J'ai reçu beaucoup de cadeaux.	I received lots of presents.
Ma sœur a eu son premier bébé.	My sister had her first baby.
Je suis allé(e) au mariage de (ma cousine).	I went to (my cousin's) wedding.
Mon frère s'est pacsé avec son compagnon.	My brother entered into a civil partnership with his partner.
Il y avait …	There was/were …
beaucoup d'invités	lots of guests
un gâteau spécial	a special cake
C'était …	It was …
génial	great

Had a look ☐ **Nearly there** ☐ **Nailed it** ☐

Extra words I should know for reading and listening activities

On fait du shopping! / *Let's go shopping!*

Ça me déstresse!*	*It de-stresses me!*
Vous désirez?	*How can I help you?*
Avez-vous … ?	*Have you got … ?*
Ça fait combien?	*How much is that?*
Je prends …	*I'll have …*
Je suis désolé(e) …	*I'm sorry …*
Je n'en ai plus.	*I haven't got any more.*
Alors …	*Well/So …*
Bien sûr.	*Of course.*
Ça fait (huit) euros, s'il vous plaît.	*That's (eight) euros, please.*

Had a look ☐ **Nearly there** ☐ **Nailed it** ☐

Les fêtes en France / *Festivals/Parties in France*

On colle un poisson dans le dos de quelqu'un.**	*We stick a fish onto someone's back.*
On dit («Poisson d'avril!»).**	*We say ("April Fool's Day!").*
On mange …	*We eat …*
Comme dessert …	*As a dessert …*
J'adore/J'aime fêter mon anniversaire.	*I love/like celebrating my birthday.*
Je reçois beaucoup de cadeaux.	*I get lots of presents.*
À part (Noël) …	*Apart from (Christmas) …*
Je suis né(e) (en août).	*I was born (in August).*
Le jour de (mon anniversaire) …	*The day of (my birthday) …*
C'est l'occasion de dire merci à (sa maman).	*It's the time to say thank you to (your mum).*
Je suis (très) romantique.	*I am (very) romantic.*
Une de mes fêtes préférées, c'est …	*One of my favourite festivals is …*
J'aime m'habiller bien.	*I like to dress well.*
le compte à rebours	*the countdown*
Tout le monde s'embrasse.*	*Everyone kisses each other.*

Had a look ☐ **Nearly there** ☐ **Nailed it** ☐

Un repas spécial / *A special meal*

Je vais m'occuper (du dessert).	*I'll take care of (the dessert).*
Je viens!	*I'm coming!*
Je vais chercher (le pain).	*I'm going to get (the bread).*
Je vais faire cuire (des morceaux de poulet).	*I'm going to cook (chicken pieces).*
Compte sur nous!	*Count on us!*
On va préparer/boire …	*We are going to prepare/drink …*
On va acheter à boire!	*We are going to buy the drinks.*
Des (grandes) bouteilles de …	*(Big) bottles of …*
On mange chez mes grands-parents/nous.	*We eat at my grand-parents' house/our house.*
Cette année/fois …	*This year/time …*
Je vais inviter toute ma famille (à un barbecue).	*I'm going to invite all of my family (to a barbecue).*
La ville où on habite …	*The town where we live …*
Je (ne) peux (pas) aller au supermarché.	*I can('t) go to the supermarket.*
Je dois acheter les provisions dans des magasins indépendants.	*I have to get the food from small/independent shops.*
Avec ça, je vais servir …	*I'm going to serve … with that.*

Had a look ☐ **Nearly there** ☐ **Nailed it** ☐

Felicitations! / *Congratulations!*

Il y avait beaucoup d'invités.	*There were lots of people invited.*
J'ai pris des photos.	*I took some photos.*
la cérémonie	*the ceremony*
le vin d'honneur	*drinks reception*
un croquembouche**	*special (wedding) cake, made of profiteroles and cream*
J'ai fêté …	*I celebrated …*
C'était une (excellente) soirée!	*It was a (great) night!*

Had a look ☐ **Nearly there** ☐ **Nailed it** ☐

*Use cognates/near cognates to work out new words and phrases such as *Ça me déstresse!* or *Tout le monde s'embrasse!*

**Some French customs are different to English ones, such as the cake served at weddings. Make a list in French and English and learn them.

Words I should know for speaking and writing activities

Où habites-tu? / *Where do you live?*

J'habite … / *I live …*
dans une ville/un village / *in a town/village*
au centre-ville / *in the town centre*
au bord de la mer / *at the seaside*
à la campagne/montagne / *in the countryside/mountains*
en ville / *in town*
à Londres/Manchester, etc. / *in London/Manchester, etc.*
dans le nord/le sud/l'est/l'ouest … / *in the north/south/east/west …*
dans le centre … / *in the centre …*
de l'Angleterre/Écosse/Irlande (du Nord) / *of England/Scotland/(Northern) Ireland*
de la France / *of France*
du pays de Galles / *of Wales*

Had a look ☐ **Nearly there** ☐ **Nailed it** ☐

Qu'est-ce qu'on peut faire? / *What can you do?*

On peut … / *You can …*
aller à un match de foot / *go to a football match*
aller au cinéma / *go to the cinema*
faire du cheval / *go horse-riding*
faire du ski / *go skiing*
faire du snowboard / *go snowboarding*
faire des promenades / *go for walks*
faire les magasins / *go shopping*
se baigner dans la mer / *swim/bathe in the sea*
se détendre sur la plage / *relax on the beach*
visiter le château / *visit the castle*
visiter les musées / *visit the museums*

Had a look ☐ **Nearly there** ☐ **Nailed it** ☐

Dans ma ville/mon village / *In my town/village*

Dans ma ville/mon village, il y a … / *In my town/village, there is/are …*
un bureau de poste/une poste / *a post office*
un centre de loisirs / *a leisure centre*
un château / *a castle*
un marché / *a market*
un musée / *a museum*
un parc/jardin public / *a park*
un stade / *a stadium*
un supermarché / *a supermarket*
une bibliothèque / *a library*
une église / *a church*
une gare (SNCF) / *a (railway) station*
une mosquée / *a mosque*
des hôtels (m) / *some hotels*

des restaurants (m) / *some restaurants*
Il n'y a pas de … / *There isn't a/aren't any …*

Had a look ☐ **Nearly there** ☐ **Nailed it** ☐

Les directions / *Directions*

Où est le/la/l' … ? / *Where is the … ?*
Où sont les … ? / *Where are the … ?*
Pour aller au/à la/à l'/aux … ? / *How do I get to the … ?*
Va/Allez tout droit. / *Go straight on.*
Tourne/Tournez à gauche/droite. / *Turn left/right.*
Prends/Prenez la première/deuxième/troisième rue à gauche/droite. / *Take the first/second/third street on the left/right.*
Traverse/Traversez le pont/la place. / *Cross the bridge/square.*
Descends/Descendez la rue. / *Go down the street.*
C'est près/loin? / *Is it near/far?*
C'est tout près/assez loin. / *It's very near/quite far.*

Had a look ☐ **Nearly there** ☐ **Nailed it** ☐

Qu'est-ce qu'il y a dans ta région? / *What is there in your region?*

Dans ma région, il y a … / *In my region there is/are …*
un lac / *a lake*
un port de pêche / *a fishing port*
une rivière/un fleuve / *a river*
des champs (m) / *fields*
des collines (f) / *hills*
des fermes (f) / *farms*
des forêts (f) / *forests*
des stations de ski (f) / *ski resorts*
des vignobles (m) / *vineyards*
En Bretagne, il y a … / *In Brittany there is/are …*
un beau château / *a beautiful castle*
une belle cathédrale / *a beautiful cathedral*
des villes historiques / *historical towns*
de vieilles maisons / *old houses*
de vieux bâtiments / *old buildings*
On peut … / *You can …*
faire de la voile / *go sailing*
faire des randonnées à vélo / *go for bike rides*

Had a look ☐ **Nearly there** ☐ **Nailed it** ☐

Le meilleur … / *The best …*

le meilleur climat / *the best climate*
la meilleure équipe de football / *the best football team*

le plus beau paysage	the most beautiful countryside
les plus belles plages	the most beautiful beaches
le plus long fleuve	the longest river
la plus longue piste de ski	the longest ski slope
la plus haute tour	the highest tower
le musée le plus populaire	the most popular museum
la région la plus historique	the most historical region
les stations de ski (f) les plus populaires	the most popular ski resorts
les monuments (m) les plus célèbres	the most famous monuments

Had a look ☐ **Nearly there** ☐ **Nailed it** ☐

Visiter une ville / Visiting a town

Je voudrais visiter/ voir …	I would like to visit/see …
Je ne voudrais pas rater …	I wouldn't want to miss …
l'aquarium (m)	the aquarium
l'exposition (f) sur …	the exhibition on …
le spectacle son et lumière	the sound and light show
Je voudrais louer des vélos.	I would like to hire bikes.
J'aimerais …	I would like …
faire une promenade en bateau	to go on a boat trip
monter à la tour de l'horloge	to climb the clock tower

Had a look ☐ **Nearly there** ☐ **Nailed it** ☐

Les renseignements touristiques / Tourist information

(Le château) est ouvert quels jours de la semaine?	On what days is (the castle) open?
C'est ouvert (tous les jours/tous les jours sauf le dimanche).	It's open (every day/every day except Sundays).
Quels sont les horaires d'ouverture?	What are the opening hours?
C'est ouvert de (9h) à (17h).	It's open from (9 a.m.) until (5 p.m.).
C'est combien, l'entrée?	How much is the entrance fee?
Ça coûte … pour les adultes et … pour les enfants.	It costs … for adults and … for children.
Est-ce qu'il y a un restaurant ou une cafétéria?	Is there a restaurant or a cafeteria?

Avez-vous un dépliant/ un plan de la ville?	Do you have a leaflet/a map of the town?
Où est-ce qu'on peut acheter des billets?	Where can we buy tickets?
la durée	duration
les tarifs (m)	prices
gratuit(e)	free
accessible aux personnes handicapées	accessible to disabled people
les chiens sont acceptés	dogs are welcome

Had a look ☐ **Nearly there** ☐ **Nailed it** ☐

Le temps/La météo / The weather/The weather forecast

Quel temps fait-il?	What is the weather like?
Il fait beau.	The weather is good.
Il fait mauvais.	The weather is bad.
Il fait chaud.	It's hot.
Il fait froid.	It's cold.
Il y a du soleil.	It's sunny.
Il y a du brouillard.	It's foggy.
Il y a du vent.	It's windy.
Il y a un orage.	There's a storm.
Il pleut.	It's raining.
Il neige.	It's snowing.
près de la Manche	near the Channel
sur la côte atlantique	on the Atlantic coast
sur la côte méditerranéenne	on the Mediterranean coast

Had a look ☐ **Nearly there** ☐ **Nailed it** ☐

Les projets / Plans

aujourd'hui	today
demain	tomorrow
après-demain	the day after tomorrow
ce week-end	this weekend
cette semaine	this week
S'il fait beau/mauvais (etc.), on va …	If the weather's good/bad (etc.), we're going …
aller à la pêche	to go fishing
aller à la piscine (en plein air)	to go to the (open-air) swimming pool
faire un barbecue	to have a barbecue
faire un pique-nique	to have a picnic
faire de la luge	to go tobogganing
rester à la maison	to stay at home
regarder la télé	to watch TV

Had a look ☐ **Nearly there** ☐ **Nailed it** ☐

Ville de rêve ou ville de cauchemar? / Dream town or nightmare town?

C'est …	It's …
très animé	very lively
trop tranquille	too quiet

sale	*dirty*
pollué(e)	*polluted*
triste	*sad*
Ce n'est jamais propre.	*It's never clean.*
Il y a …	*There is/are …*
de bons transports en commun	*good public transport*
seulement des maisons et une église	*only houses and a church*
trop de circulation	*too much traffic*
trop de bruit	*too much noise*
toujours des déchets par terre	*always rubbish on the ground*
Il n'y a rien pour les jeunes.	*There is nothing for young people.*
Il n'y a pas grand-chose à faire.	*There is not much to do.*
Il n'y a pas de zone piétonne.	*There is no pedestrian precinct.*
Il n'y a plus de cinéma.	*There is no longer a cinema.*
Le cinéma est fermé.	*The cinema is closed (down).*
un club pour les jeunes	*a youth club*
les poubelles (f)	*bins*
en banlieue	*in the suburbs*
le quartier	*neighbourhood, district, part of town*

Had a look ☐ **Nearly there** ☐ **Nailed it** ☐

M
4

Extra words I should know for reading and listening activities

Qu'est-ce qu'il y a où tu habites?	*What is there where you live?*	C'est comment où tu habites?	*What is it like where you live?*
des belles plages	*beautiful beaches*	tout** ...	*very ...*
des beaux châteaux	*beautiful castles*	... petit	*... small*
des grandes forêts	*large forests*	... propre	*... clean*
la capitale	*the capital*	... triste	*... sad*
la plus haute montagne de France*	*the highest mountain in France*	culturel(le)	*cultural*
		mon quartier	*my neighbourhood*
le plus grand château de France et du monde*	*The biggest castle in France and the world*	Il (n')y a ... (rien) pour les jeunes.	*There is ... (nothing) for young people.*
la meilleure équipe de foot*	*The best football team*	Il y avait ...	*There used to be ...*
		un endroit sans pollution	*a place without pollution*
		complètement	*completely*
		J'ai repondu à un sondage en ligne.	*I answered an online survey.*
		les aspects de la ville	*the aspects of the town*
		Il faut avoir ...	*You should have ...*
		Je veux habiter (dans) un endroit propre.	*I want to live in a clean place.*

Had a look ☐   **Nearly there** ☐   **Nailed it** ☐

Les renseignements touristiques	*Tourist information*
Ça, c'est plus intéressant!	*That's more interesting!*
le spectacle son et lumière	*sound and lights show*
une promenade (commentée) en bateau	*(guided) boat trip*
une randonnée à vélo	*bike ride*
les requins (m)	*sharks*
les navettes spatiales (f)	*space shuttles*
environ	*about*
l'horloge (f)	*clock tower*

Had a look ☐   **Nearly there** ☐   **Nailed it** ☐

Had a look ☐   **Nearly there** ☐   **Nailed it** ☐

Les activités	*Activities*
dans le jardin	*in the garden*
pendant les vacances	*during the holidays*

Had a look ☐   **Nearly there** ☐   **Nailed it** ☐

*Learn key geographical, cultural or historical aspects about France, such as which is the longest river, the highest mountain, etc. You can use them in the speaking exam to impress the examiner. This knowledge will also help you understand more easily passages in the reading and listening exams.

**Be very careful of words that can have more than one meaning. *Tout* can mean 'all', 'quite', 'every', 'any' and 'very'!

Another example is *de*, which depending on the context means 'from', 'of', 'some' and 'in'.

Words I should know for speaking and writing activities

Les pays — Countries
le Danemark	Denmark
le Pakistan	Pakistan
le pays de Galles	Wales
le Royaume-Uni	the UK
l'Algérie (f)	Algeria
l'Allemagne (f)	Germany
l'Angleterre (f)	England
l'Autriche (f)	Austria
la Belgique	Belgium
l'Espagne (f)	Spain
l'Italie (f)	Italy
la Pologne	Poland
la Russie	Russia
la Suisse	Switzerland
les États-Unis (m)	the USA
les Pays-Bas (m)	the Netherlands

Had a look ☐   Nearly there ☐   Nailed it ☐

Les vacances — Holidays
Où vas-tu en vacances?	Where do you go on holiday?
Je vais …	I go …
en France	to France
au pays de Galles	to Wales
aux États-Unis	to the USA
Comment voyages-tu?	How do you travel?
Je voyage …	I travel …
en avion	by plane
en bateau	by boat
en car	by coach
en train	by train
en voiture	by car
à vélo	by bike
Où loges-tu?	Where do you stay?
Je loge dans …	I stay in/on …
un camping	a campsite
un hôtel	a hotel
une auberge de jeunesse	a youth hostel
une caravane	a caravan

Had a look ☐   Nearly there ☐   Nailed it ☐

Avec qui pars-tu en vacances?	Who do you go on holiday with?
Je pars …	I go …
avec ma famille	with my family
avec mes copains/copines	with my friends
avec mes grands-parents	with my grandparents
seul(e)	alone
C'est comment?	What's it like?
C'est …	It's …

extra/formidable	amazing/great
bien	good
ennuyeux/nul	boring/rubbish
Ce n'est pas mal.	It's not bad.

Had a look ☐   Nearly there ☐   Nailed it ☐

Les hôtels — Hotels
un hôtel	a hotel
des chambres d'hôtes	guest rooms (i.e. in a B&B/guest house)
Nous proposons des chambres avec …	We offer rooms with …
un grand lit	a double bed
un lit simple	a single bed
une salle de bains	a bathroom
une douche	a shower
un micro-ondes	a microwave
une télévision à écran plat	a flat-screen TV
(une) vue sur la mer	a sea view
un balcon	a balcony
la climatisation	air conditioning

Had a look ☐   Nearly there ☐   Nailed it ☐

Nous avons aussi …	We also have …
une aire de jeux	a games area
un parking	a car park
une piscine	a swimming pool
un restaurant	a restaurant
le Wi-Fi	Wi-Fi
Nos chambres sont bien équipées.	Our rooms are well equipped.
Le petit-déjeuner est inclus/compris.	Breakfast is included.
Notre hôtel est situé/se trouve …	Our hotel is located …

Had a look ☐   Nearly there ☐   Nailed it ☐

Réserver une chambre — Booking a room
Nous voulons/Je voudrais réserver une chambre …	We want/I would like to book a room …
pour une/deux personne(s)	for one person/two people
avec un lit simple/un grand lit	with a single/double bed
pour une nuit/deux nuits	for one night/two nights
Est-ce que vous avez … ?	Do you have … ?
une piscine	a swimming pool
la climatisation	air conditioning
Votre chambre est …	Your room is …

M 5

au rez-de-chaussée	on the ground floor
au premier étage	on the first floor
au deuxième étage	on the second floor
Je voudrais payer avec ma carte bancaire.	I would like to pay with my debit/credit card.

Had a look ☐ **Nearly there** ☐ **Nailed it** ☐

Voyager — Travelling

l'aéroport (m)	airport
le billet	ticket
le conducteur/la conductrice	driver
le contrôle des passeports	passport control
le guichet	ticket office/counter
le/la pilote	pilot
le quai	platform
l'autoroute (f)	motorway
la ceinture de sécurité	seatbelt
la circulation	traffic
la douane	customs
la gare	station
la route	road
les bagages (m)	luggage

Had a look ☐ **Nearly there** ☐ **Nailed it** ☐

Au guichet — At the ticket counter

Je peux vous aider?	Can I help you?
Je voudrais un aller simple/un aller-retour pour (Lyon), s'il vous plaît.	I would like a single/a return to (Lyon), please.
En quelle classe?	In which class?
En première/deuxième classe.	In first/second class.
C'est quel quai?	Which platform is it?
Le train part à quelle heure?	What time does the train leave?
Le voyage dure combien de temps?	How long does the journey last?
Est-ce qu'il faut changer?	Do I/we have to change?
C'est un train direct.	The train is direct.

Had a look ☐ **Nearly there** ☐ **Nailed it** ☐

Moyens de transports préférés et raisons — Favourite means of transport and reasons

Je voyage toujours (en train, etc.) parce que c'est …	I always travel (by train, etc.) because it's …
plus rapide/plus confortable	faster/more comfortable
plus pratique/plus vert	more practical/greener
plus aventureux	more adventurous
mieux/meilleur pour la planète	better for the planet

moins ennuyeux/fatigant	less boring/tiring
moins cher	less expensive

Had a look ☐ **Nearly there** ☐ **Nailed it** ☐

Les activités en vacances — Holiday activities

Je fais de la planche à voile.	I go windsurfing.
Je fais de la voile.	I go sailing.
Je fais de l'accrobranche.	I do a tree-top adventure.
Je fais du ski.	I go skiing.
Je visite les musées.	I visit the museums.
Je visite les monuments.	I visit the monuments.
Je vais à la pêche.	I go fishing.
Je vais à la plage.	I go to the beach.
Je joue à la pétanque.	I play French bowls.
Je me baigne.	I swim (in the sea).
Je me promène.	I go for a walk.
Je me repose.	I rest.
Je me lève (tôt/tard).	I get up (early/late).
Je m'habille.	I get dressed.
Je ne m'ennuie pas.	I don't get bored.
Je sors au restaurant.	I go out to a restaurant.

Had a look ☐ **Nearly there** ☐ **Nailed it** ☐

Au restaurant — At the restaurant

Voici la carte.	Here is the menu.
Le plat du jour, c'est …	The daily special is …
Vous avez fait votre choix?	Have you made your choice?
Pour commencer, je vais prendre …	To start, I am going to have …
Comme plat principal, je voudrais …	As a main course, I would like …
Je vais prendre le menu (à 30 euros).	I am going to have the (30 euro) set menu.
Et comme boisson?	And to drink?
Qu'est-ce que vous avez comme desserts?	What desserts do you have?
Vous avez besoin d'autre chose?	Do you need anything else?
On a besoin de l'addition.	We need the bill.
J'ai faim.	I am hungry.
J'ai soif.	I am thirsty.
J'ai envie d'un dessert.	I want a dessert.

Had a look ☐ **Nearly there** ☐ **Nailed it** ☐

Les plats — Dishes

les entrées (f)	starters
les brochettes (f) de crevettes (f)	prawn skewers
les escargots (m)	snails
la soupe à la tomate	tomato soup

la tarte à l'oignon	onion tart
les plats principaux (m)	main dishes
l'épaule d'agneau (f)	shoulder of lamb
la cuisse de canard	duck leg
les lasagnes végétariennes (f)	vegetarian lasagne
le loup de mer	sea bass
le poulet basquaise	Basque-style chicken
le rôti de veau	roast veal
les desserts (m)	desserts
la crème brûlée	crème brûlée
la mousse au chocolat	chocolate mousse
le roulé au chocolat	chocolate roll
le sorbet	sorbet
la tarte au citron	lemon tart
la tarte aux pommes	apple tart
l'eau gazeuse (f)	sparkling water

Had a look ☐ **Nearly there** ☐ **Nailed it** ☐

Critiques / Reviews

J'y suis allé(e) pour le déjeuner/le dîner.	I went there for lunch/dinner.
Le service était lent/exceptionnel.	The service was slow/exceptional.
Le serveur/La serveuse était/n'était pas (très) poli(e).	The waiter/waitress was/wasn't (very) polite.
C'était …	It was …
délicieux/bien cuit.	delicious/well-cooked.
La nourriture était froide/trop salée.	The food was cold/too salty.
La nourriture n'était pas cuite.	The food wasn't cooked.
Je recommande/Je ne recommande pas ce restaurant.	I recommend/don't recommend this restaurant.

Had a look ☐ **Nearly there** ☐ **Nailed it** ☐

Des vacances catastrophiques / Catastrophic holidays

J'ai oublié mon passeport.	I forgot my passport.
J'ai pris un coup de soleil.	I got sunburnt.
J'ai cassé mon appareil photo.	I broke my camera.
J'ai été malade.	I got sick.
On m'a volé mon sac.	Someone stole my handbag.
Il a plu tous les jours.	It rained every day.
Il y avait des cafards dans notre chambre.	There were cockroaches in our room.
J'ai raté l'avion.	I missed the plane.
J'ai dû aller chez le médecin.	I had to go to the doctor.
J'ai perdu mes photos.	I lost my photos.
J'ai vomi.	I vomited.
J'ai dû aller au commissariat.	I had to go to the police station.
Il n'y avait rien à faire.	There was nothing to do.
On a dû chercher un autre hôtel.	We had to look for another hotel.
La prochaine fois, je vais …	Next time, I am going …
faire plus attention	to be more careful
mettre de la crème solaire	to put on sun cream
loger dans un camping	to stay on a campsite

Had a look ☐ **Nearly there** ☐ **Nailed it** ☐

M
5

33

Extra words I should know for reading and listening activities

L'hébergement — *Accommodation*

un hôtel familial/de luxe au bord du fleuve	*a family/luxury hotel by the river*
un hôtel 4 étoiles prêt à vous accueillir	*a four-star hotel ready to welcome you*
spacieux/-euse(s)	*spacious*
notre maison	*our house*
au premier/deuxième étage	*on the first/second floor*
un parking à votre disposition	*a car park for you*
tout de suite	*straightaway*
une salle de bains privée	*a private bathroom*
une piscine extérieure	*an outdoor swimming pool*
toutes les formules possibles	*all possible options*
une aire de jeux	*a play area*
confortable/parfait	*comfortable/perfect*
Nous mettons …	*We put …*
Nous proposons …	*We offer …*
Nous avons une chambre pour … personnes(s).	*We have a room for … people.*
bien situé(e)	*well-situated*
dormir	*to sleep*
ouvert(e)/fermé(e) toute l'année	*open/closed all year*

Had a look ☐ **Nearly there** ☐ **Nailed it** ☐

Pour réserver un hôtel — *To reserve a hotel*

(Comment) voulez-vous (payer)?	*(How) do you want (to pay)?*
Quelle sorte de … ?	*What type of … ?*
Combien de nuits?	*How many nights?*

Had a look ☐ **Nearly there** ☐ **Nailed it** ☐

En route! — *On the road!*

(Le train) arrive à quelle heure?	*What time does (the train) arrive?*
Bon voyage!	*Have a good trip!*
Je vais (aller) …*	*I go/am going (to go) …*
J'y vais …	*I go there …*
J'aime (beaucoup) …	*I (really) like …*
prendre l'avion	*to take the plane*
(y) aller en ferry	*to go by ferry*
rencontrer des gens	*to meet people*
voyager en voiture	*to travel by car*
faire du vélo	*to go cycling*
C'est tout simplement la classe!	*It's simply awesome!*
Quand y vas-tu?	*When do you go?*
tous les ans	*every year*
le lendemain	*the day after tomorrow*
C'est (nettement) mieux.	*It's (clearly) better.*

en (juillet)	*in (July)*
Que fais-tu?	*What do you do?*

Had a look ☐ **Nearly there** ☐ **Nailed it** ☐

Les vacances de l'année dernière — *Last year's holidays*

C'était mon premier/dernier jour de vacances.	*It was my first/last day of the holidays.*
J'ai décidé de …	*I decided to …*
Je me suis levé(e) …	*I got up …*
très tôt	*very early*
tard	*late*
à midi	*at midday*
Je suis allé(e) …	*I went …*
à la plage	*to the beach*
en boîte	*to a nightclub*
J'ai retrouvé des amis …	*I met friends …*
J'ai vu le lever du soleil.	*I saw the sunrise.*
J'ai dansé au soleil/sous le soleil.	*I danced in the sun.*
Qu'est-ce que c'était beau!	*How beautiful it was!*

Had a look ☐ **Nearly there** ☐ **Nailed it** ☐

Bon appétit! — *Enjoy your food!*

Pour commencer, je vais prendre …	*To start, I am going to have …*
Pour moi …	*For me …*
J'ai (très) faim.	*I'm (very) hungry.*
Vous avez besoin d'autre chose?	*Would you like anything else?*
L'addition, s'il vous plaît.	*The bill, please.*
C'était froid/parfait/délicieux.	*It was cold/perfect/delicious.*

Had a look ☐ **Nearly there** ☐ **Nailed it** ☐

Les catastrophes! — *Catastrophes!*

Quel dommage!	*What a shame!*
J'ai passé une nuit dans un hôtel sale.	*I spent a night in a dirty hotel.*
Il y avait une odeur bizarre.	*There was a strange smell.*
La salle de bains n'était pas propre non plus!	*The bathroom wasn't clean either!*
La climatisation était cassée.	*The air conditionning was broken.*

Had a look ☐ **Nearly there** ☐ **Nailed it** ☐

⭐ *Je fais … and Je vais … can both be translated as 'I go …'. However, you can only use Je vais … to mean 'I go …' with a destination. Je fais … only means 'I go …' when it is with a sport, for example: Je fais de la natation. I go swimming.

34

Words I should know for speaking and writing activities

Les matières	School subjects
le commerce	business studies
le dessin	art
le français	French
la biologie	biology
la chimie	chemistry
la géographie	geography
la musique	music
la physique	physics
la religion	religious studies
la technologie	technology
l'allemand (m)	German
l'anglais (m)	English
l'art dramatique (m)	drama
le théâtre	drama
l'EPS (f)/le sport	PE
l'espagnol (m)	Spanish
l'étude des médias (f)	media studies
l'histoire (f)	history
l'informatique (f)	ICT
l'instruction civique (f)	citizenship
les arts ménagers (m)	home technology
les maths (m)	maths

Had a look ☐ **Nearly there** ☐ **Nailed it** ☐

L'emploi du temps	The timetable
à neuf heures	at nine o'clock
à neuf heures dix	at ten past nine
à neuf heures et quart	at a quarter past nine
à neuf heures et demie	at half past nine
à dix heures moins vingt	at twenty to ten
à dix heures moins le quart	at a quarter to ten
lundi	(on) Monday(s)
mardi	(on) Tuesday(s)
mercredi	(on) Wednesday(s)
jeudi	(on) Thursday(s)
vendredi	(on) Friday(s)
la récré(ation)	break time
l'heure du déjeuner	lunchtime
Lundi à neuf heures, j'ai histoire.	On Monday at nine o'clock, I have history.
Vendredi, j'ai deux heures de français.	I have two French lessons on Fridays.
La récré commence à …	Break time starts at …

Had a look ☐ **Nearly there** ☐ **Nailed it** ☐

Ce que j'aime et ce que je n'aime pas	What I like and what I don't like
Ma matière préférée est …	My favourite subject is …
je suis fort(e) en …	I am good at …
je suis faible en …	I am weak at …
je (ne) suis (pas) doué(e) en …	I (don't) have a talent for …

C'est …	It's …
facile/difficile	easy/difficult
utile/inutile	useful/useless
intéressant/ennuyeux	interesting/boring
fascinant/passionnant	fascinating/exciting
Le/La prof est …	The teacher is …
bon(ne)/marrant(e)	good/funny
sympa/gentil(le)	nice/kind
sévère/impatient(e)	strict/impatient
On a trop de devoirs.	We have too much homework.

Had a look ☐ **Nearly there** ☐ **Nailed it** ☐

Une école bien équipée	A well-equipped school
le gymnase	sports hall
le hall	(assembly) hall, auditorium
le terrain de basket	basketball court
le terrain de sport	sports ground
la bibliothèque	library
la cantine	canteen
la cour de récréation	playground
la piscine	swimming pool
la salle de sport	gym
les labos de science (m)	science labs
les salles de classe (f)	classrooms
les vestiaires (m)	changing rooms

Had a look ☐ **Nearly there** ☐ **Nailed it** ☐

Mon collège	My school
Comment s'appelle ton école?	What is your school called?
Mon école s'appelle …	My school is called …
C'est quelle sorte d'école?	What sort of school is it?
C'est …	It's …
une école mixte	a mixed school
une école publique	a state school
une école privée	a private school
une école pour filles/garçons	a school for girls/boys
pour les élèves de 11 à 16 ans	for pupils aged 11 to 16
Il y a combien d'élèves?	How many pupils are there?
Il y a (750) élèves et (45) professeurs.	There are (750) pupils and (45) teachers.
Quels sont les horaires?	What are the school hours?
La journée commence à (8h30) et finit à (16h ou à 17h).	The school day starts at (8.30 a.m.) and finishes at (4 or 5 p.m.).
Il y a combien de cours par jour?	How many lessons are there per day?
Il y a (huit) cours par jour.	There are (eight) lessons per day.

M 6

35

Comment sont les professeurs? — *What are the teachers like?*

En général, les profs sont gentils/un peu sévères. — *In general, teachers are kind/a bit strict.*

Qu'est-ce que tu penses de ton collège? — *What do you think of your school?*

Je pense que les journées sont longues et qu'on a trop de contrôles. — *I think the days are long and we have too many tests.*

Had a look ☐   **Nearly there** ☐   **Nailed it** ☐

L'école chez nous, l'école chez vous
School here and with you

En Grande-Bretagne, … — *In Britain …*

En France, … — *In France …*

l'école commence à … et finit à … — *school starts at … and finishes at …*

on porte un uniforme scolaire — *we wear school uniform*

ils portent leurs propres habits — *they wear their own clothes*

on étudie la religion — *we study RE*

ils n'étudient pas la religion — *they don't study RE*

on ne redouble pas — *we don't repeat a year*

ils redoublent — *they repeat a year*

les grandes vacances durent … — *the summer holidays last …*

Je préfère le système britannique/français parce que … — *I prefer the British/French system because …*

le redoublement (n')est (pas) une bonne idée — *repeating a year is (not) a good idea*

les horaires sont plus raisonnables — *the hours are more reasonable*

les vacances sont plus longues — *the holidays are longer*

l'uniforme scolaire est pratique — *school uniform is practical*

Had a look ☐   **Nearly there** ☐   **Nailed it** ☐

Le règlement scolaire
School rules

Il faut être à l'heure. — *You must be on time.*

Il faut faire ses devoirs. — *You have to do your homework.*

Il faut porter l'uniforme scolaire. — *You have to wear school uniform.*

Il est interdit de mâcher du chewing-gum. — *It is forbidden to chew gum.*

Il est interdit d'utiliser son portable en classe. — *It is forbidden to use your mobile phone in class.*

Il est interdit de porter des bijoux, des piercings ou trop de maquillage. — *It is forbidden to wear jewellery, piercings or too much make-up.*

Il est interdit de sortir de l'école pendant l'heure du déjeuner. — *It is forbidden to leave school at lunchtime.*

Il est interdit de manquer les cours. — *It is forbidden to skip lessons.*

Je trouve ça … — *I think that's …*

juste/logique — *fair/logical*

raisonnable/frustrant(e) — *reasonable/frustrating*

injuste/ridicule — *unfair/ridiculous*

Had a look ☐   **Nearly there** ☐   **Nailed it** ☐

parce que/car … — *because …*

c'est/ce n'est pas dangereux — *it is/isn't dangerous*

c'est/ce n'est pas important — *it is/isn't important*

on n'est pas des bébés — *we aren't babies*

il faut respecter les autres — *you have to respect other people*

la mode/la religion n'a pas de place à l'école — *fashion/religion doesn't have any place in school*

l'école, c'est pour apprendre — *school is for learning*

Had a look ☐   **Nearly there** ☐   **Nailed it** ☐

L'uniforme scolaire
School uniform

Je porte … — *I wear …*

un pantalon/un polo — *trousers/a polo shirt*

un sweat/une chemise — *a sweatshirt/a shirt*

une cravate/une jupe — *a tie/a skirt*

une veste — *a blazer/jacket*

mes propres vêtements (m) — *my own clothes*

La mode n'a pas de place à l'école. — *Fashion has no place in school.*

L'uniforme coûte cher. — *Uniform is expensive.*

Tout le monde se ressemble. — *Everyone looks the same/alike.*

C'est démodé et embarrassant. — *It's old-fashioned and embarrassing.*

C'est pratique et confortable. — *It's practical and comfortable.*

Had a look ☐   **Nearly there** ☐   **Nailed it** ☐

La santé au collège
Health at school

Pour être en pleine forme, … — *To be healthy, …*

Pour éviter le stress au collège, … — *To avoid stress at school, …*

je mange sainement — *I eat healthily*

je mange rarement des bonbons ou des gâteaux — *I rarely eat sweets or cakes*

je bois uniquement de l'eau — *I only drink water*

je ne bois jamais de boissons gazeuses — *I never drink fizzy drinks*

je me couche tôt	I go to bed early
j'essaie de me déconnecter des écrans de temps en temps	I try to disconnect from screens from time to time

Had a look ☐ **Nearly there** ☐ **Nailed it** ☐

Je m'inquiète pour (mon copain/ma sœur).	I am worried about (my friend/my sister).
Il/Elle …	He/She …
fume des cigarettes	smokes cigarettes
fume du cannabis	smokes cannabis
boit de l'alcool	drinks alcohol
ne mange pas sainement	doesn't eat healthily
Il/Elle fait ça pour …	He/She does that …
s'amuser	to have fun
faire partie du groupe	to be part of a group
combattre le stress au collège	to combat/to deal with stress at school
perdre du poids	to lose weight
Il/Elle …	He/She …
est moins sociable	is less sociable
ne peut pas se concentrer en classe	can't concentrate in class
va avoir de mauvaises notes	is going to have bad grades
va devenir anorexique	is going to become anorexic
À mon avis, c'est …	In my opinion, it's …
très mauvais pour la santé	very bad for your health
dangereux/illégal	dangerous/illegal
On devient facilement accro.	You become addicted easily.

Had a look ☐ **Nearly there** ☐ **Nailed it** ☐

À l'école primaire et maintenant / At primary school and now

J'avais …	I had/used to have …
J'ai …	I have …
beaucoup de temps libre	lots of free time
beaucoup d'amis	lots of friends
trop de devoirs	too much homework
J'allais …	I used to go …
Je vais …	I go …
au ciné-club	to film club
au club d'échecs	to chess club
au zoo	to the zoo
à la piscine	to the swimming pool
J'étais …	I was/used to be …
Je suis …	I am …
dans une chorale	in a choir
délégué(e) de classe	class representative
membre de l'équipe de basket	a member of the basketball team
timide	shy

Had a look ☐ **Nearly there** ☐ **Nailed it** ☐

Je faisais …	I used to do/go …
Je fais …	I do/go …
du judo/du karaté	judo/karate
du yoga/de la danse	yoga/dancing
de la natation	swimming
Je jouais …	I used to play …
Je joue …	I play …
à cache-cache	hide and seek
au foot/au hand	football/handball
au ping-pong	ping pong, table tennis
au rugby	rugby
Je participais …	I used to participate/take part …
Je participe …	I participate/take part …
au spectacle de Noël	in the Christmas play
Je chantais …	I sang …
Je chante …	I sing …
dans la chorale	in the choir

Had a look ☐ **Nearly there** ☐ **Nailed it** ☐

Les succès au collège / Successes at school

Je suis fier/-ière de moi.	I am proud of myself.
Je joue dans l'orchestre.	I play in the orchestra.
Je suis membre du club informatique.	I'm a member of the IT club.
Je suis membre du conseil d'administration.	I'm a member of the school council.
Je vais jouer dans l'équipe de hockey.	I'm going to play in the hockey team.
Je vais participer à un échange scolaire.	I'm going to take part in a school exchange.
J'ai gagné …	I won …
un prix pour mes efforts en classe	a prize for my efforts in class
le championnat de foot/basket	the football/basketball championship
un concours de slam/danse	a slam/dance competition

Had a look ☐ **Nearly there** ☐ **Nailed it** ☐

J'ai participé à …	I participated/took part in …
un spectacle	a show
un échange scolaire	a school exchange
une sortie scolaire	a school visit
J'ai organisé …	I organised …
un concert	a concert
un concours de chant	a singing competition
J'ai récolté de l'argent pour une association caritative.	I raised money for a charity.
Les sorties scolaires sont une bonne/mauvaise idée parce que/qu' …	School visits are a good/bad idea because …
on se fait de nouveaux amis	you make new friends
on s'amuse ensemble	you have a laugh together
c'est trop cher/ennuyeux	it's too expensive/boring

Had a look ☐ **Nearly there** ☐ **Nailed it** ☐

M 6

Extra words I should know for reading and listening activities

Mes matières et mes profs
My subjects and my teachers

Mon/Ma prof s'appelle …	*My teacher is called …*
Les profs (de maths) sont …	*The (maths) teachers are …*
Je le/la/les déteste.	*I hate him/her/them.*
Je l'/les adore.	*I love him/her/them.*
Je pense que … est (trop/très/assez/un peu) …	*I think that … is (too/very/quite/a little) …*
C'est amusant/excellent.	*It is fun/excellent.*

Had a look ☐ **Nearly there** ☐ **Nailed it** ☐

Dans mon collège
In my school

Il y a (environ) …	*There is/are (about) …*
Malheureusement, il n'y a pas de …	*Unfortunately, there isn't/ aren't …*
des salles de classes modernes (f)	*modern classrooms*
une grande cour de récréation	*a big playground*
un grand choix de …	*a great choice of …*
un labo(ratoire) de langues/sciences	*a language/science laboratory*
un gymnase immense	*a huge gym*
Les vestiaires/les toilettes sont sales/sont pleins de …	*The changing rooms/ toilets are dirty/full of …*
Je le/la/les trouve bien/utile(s)/cool/bien aménagé(es).	*I think it is/they are good/useful/cool/well-equipped.*

Had a look ☐ **Nearly there** ☐ **Nailed it** ☐

Les études en Angleterre et en France
Studying in France and in England

Les cours commencent/finissent à … heure(s).	*Lessons start/end at … o'clock.*
La récré est à … et dure … minutes.	*Break starts at … and lasts … minutes.*
Il y a … cours par jour/élèves/contrôles.	*There are … lessons per day/pupils/tests.*
Il n'y a pas cours le …	*There are no lessons on …*
On a … heure(s) pour le déjeuner.	*We have … hour(s) for lunch.*
On a trop de …	*We have too many …*
Les journées/cours sont (trop) …	*The days/lessons are (too) …*
un lycée	*a high school (Yr 11-13 only)*
En sixième/cinquième/quatrième/troisième/seconde*/première*/terminale*	*In Yr 7/8/9/10/11/12/13*
à l'âge de … ans	*at the age of … years old*

après le collège	*after middle/high school*
S'ils ne font pas assez de progrès, ils redoublent**.	*If they do not make enough progress, they repeat the year.*
Les élèves passent leur brevet du collège/baccalauréat/en classe supérieure.	*The pupils take their GCSEs/A Levels/move up to the next class.*
Les élèves continuent leurs études à l'université.	*The pupils continue their studies at university.*
Les grandes vacances durent … semaines/mois.	*The summer holidays last … weeks/months.*

Had a look ☐ **Nearly there** ☐ **Nailed it** ☐

L'uniforme scolaire
School uniform

le jean	*jeans*
le jogging	*jogging pants*
le pull	*a jumper*
le tee-shirt	*t-shirt*
La mode/L'uniforme coûte cher.	*Fashion/The uniform is expensive.*
La mode n'a pas de place …	*Fashion has no place …*
se ressembler	*to look like each other*
Je (ne) voudrais (pas) …	*I would (not) like …*
C'est démodé.	*It's old-fashioned.*
C'est pratique.	*It's practical.*
C'est confortable.	*It's confortable.*
C'est embarrassant.	*It's embarrassing.*

Had a look ☐ **Nearly there** ☐ **Nailed it** ☐

La vie extra-scolaire
After-school activities

l'orchestre (m)	*the orchestra*
faire du théâtre/beaucoup de clubs	*to do drama/lots of clubs*
aller à la piscine municipale	*to go to the local pool*

Had a look ☐ **Nearly there** ☐ **Nailed it** ☐

Être en pleine forme
To be healthy

J'essaie de manger cinq portions de fruits et légumes.	*I try to eat five portions of fruit and vegetables.*
Je (ne) mange (pas) bien/assez le matin.	*I (don't) eat well/enough in the morning.*
Un bon petit-déjeuner est essentiel.	*A good breakfast is essential.*
Pour éviter le stress …	*To avoid stress …*
Je fais du sport régulièrement.	*I do sport regularly.*

M 6

Quand je dors mal/bien …	When I sleep badly/well …
Avant de dormir …	Before going to bed …
Avant d'aller au collège …	Before going to school …
Je suis (trop) fatigué(e) pour apprendre.	I am (too) tired to learn.

Had a look ☐ **Nearly there** ☐ **Nailed it** ☐

Je vais/On va participer au concours de …	I am going/We are going to participate in a … competition.
Je vais/On va voir une pièce de théâtre.	I am going/We are going to see a play.

Had a look ☐ **Nearly there** ☐ **Nailed it** ☐

Les soucis / Worries

Il/Elle fume.	He/She smokes.
Il/Elle fait énormement de sport.	He/She does lots of sport.
perdre du poids	to lose weight
J'ai peur!	I'm scared!
Je pense que …	I think that …
Il/Elle a de nouveaux copains/nouvelles copines.	He/She has new friends.
Il/Elle est plus/moins …	He/She is more/less …
Il/Elle va avoir de mauvaises notes*.	He/She is going to get bad grades.

Had a look ☐ **Nearly there** ☐ **Nailed it** ☐

Qu'est-ce que tu fais pour ton collège? / What do you do for your school?

Je représente ma classe.	I represent my class.
On discute des problèmes au collège.	We discuss problems at school.
On organise des activités.	We organise activities.
On a organisé un concours de (slam).	We organised a (slam) competition.
On a joué contre une équipe de …	We played against a team from …
On a gagné le match.	We won the match.
J'ai fait/Je vais faire un échange.	I did/I am going to do an exchange.
J'ai parlé …	I spoke …

M
6

⭐ *Watch out for false friends such as *seconde*, *première* and *terminale*. In the context of school, all of these words have very specific meanings: Year 11, Year 12 and Year 13.

Learn as many as you can, such as *les notes* (marks/grades), so that you avoid mistranslating phrases.

⭐ **Redoubler* in a school context does not mean 'to redouble'. It conveys the idea of repeating a school year, which is something French pupils have to do if they don't make sufficient progress over the year! It is important that you learn how the French education system works as it is very different to the English one.

Words I should know for speaking and writing activities

Les métiers / *Jobs*

Je suis/Il/Elle est … — *I am/He/She is a/an …*
Je veux être … — *I want to be a/an …*
Je veux travailler comme … — *I want to work as a/an …*

avocat/avocate	*lawyer*
ingénieur/ingénieure	*engineer*
électricien/électricienne	*electrician*
mécanicien/mécanicienne	*mechanic*
musicien/musicienne	*musician*
maçon/maçonne	*builder*
patron/patronne	*boss*
coiffeur/coiffeuse	*hairdresser*
programmeur/programmeuse	*computer programmer*
serveur/serveuse	*waiter/waitress*
vendeur/vendeuse	*salesperson*
acteur/actrice	*actor/actress*
agriculteur/agricultrice	*farmer*
créateur/créatrice de mode	*fashion designer*
créateur/créatrice de jeux vidéo	*video game designer*
directeur/directrice d'entreprise	*company director*
facteur/factrice	*postman/woman*

Had a look ☐ Nearly there ☐ Nailed it ☐

instituteur/institutrice	*primary school teacher*
boucher/bouchère	*butcher*
boulanger/boulangère	*baker*
fermier/fermière	*farmer*
infirmier/infirmière	*nurse*
pompier/pompière	*firefighter*
architecte	*architect*
chef de cuisine	*chef*
comptable	*accountant*
dentiste	*dentist*
journaliste	*journalist*
pilote	*pilot*
secrétaire	*secretary*
vétérinaire	*vet*
agent de police	*policeman/woman*
médecin	*doctor*
professeur	*teacher*
soldat	*soldier*

Had a look ☐ Nearly there ☐ Nailed it ☐

Lieux de travail / *Workplaces*

Je travaille/Il/Elle travaille … — *I work/He/She works …*

dans un bureau	*in an office*
dans un commissariat de police	*in a police station*
dans un collège	*in a secondary school*
dans un garage	*in a garage*
dans un hôpital	*in a hospital*
dans un magasin	*in a shop*
dans un restaurant	*in a restaurant*
dans un salon de coiffure	*in a hair salon*
dans une boulangerie	*in a bakery*
dans une école primaire	*in a primary school*
dans une ferme	*on a farm*
à bord d'un avion	*on a plane*

Had a look ☐ Nearly there ☐ Nailed it ☐

Les passions / *Passions*

Ma passion, c'est … — *My passion is …*

la cuisine/la mode	*cooking/fashion*
le sport/le théâtre	*sport/theatre/drama*
les ordinateurs (m)/les voitures (f)	*computers/cars*

Had a look ☐ Nearly there ☐ Nailed it ☐

J'aimerais … / *I would like to …*

Je voudrais/J'aimerais travailler … — *I would like to work …*

dans un bureau	*in an office*
dans un magasin	*in a shop*
en plein air	*outside*
avec des enfants	*with children*
avec des animaux	*with animals*
avec des ordinateurs	*with computers*
seul(e)	*alone, on my own*
en équipe	*in a team*
à l'étranger	*abroad*

Je voudrais faire un métier … — *I would like to do a … job*

créatif	*creative*
manuel	*manual*
à responsabilité	*responsible, with responsibility/management*

Had a look ☐ Nearly there ☐ Nailed it ☐

Tu voudrais travailler dans quel secteur et pourquoi? / *What area would you like to work in and why?*

Je voudrais travailler dans … — *I would like to work in …*

le sport et les loisirs	*sport and leisure*
le commerce	*business*
la médecine et la santé	*medicine and health*
l'audiovisuel et les médias	*audiovisual and media*

M 7

l'informatique et les télécommunications	IT and telecommunications
l'hôtellerie et la restauration	the hotel and catering industry

Had a look ☐ **Nearly there** ☐ **Nailed it** ☐

Je suis …	I am …
indépendant(e)	independent
intelligent(e)	intelligent
motivé(e)	motivated
(bien) organisé(e)	(well-)organised
actif/-ve	active
créatif/-ve	creative
ambitieux/-euse	ambitious
sérieux/-euse	serious
travailleur/-euse	hard-working
sociable	sociable
timide	shy
J'aime …	I like …
le contact avec les gens	(having) contact with people
travailler en équipe	working in a team
J'aimerais avoir un métier bien payé.	I would like to have a well-paid job.

Had a look ☐ **Nearly there** ☐ **Nailed it** ☐

Mes projets d'avenir — My plans for the future

Je veux/J'espère/Je voudrais …	I want/I hope/I would like …
passer mes examens	to take my exams
réussir mes examens	to pass my exams
prendre une année sabbatique	to take a gap year
voyager/visiter d'autres pays	to travel/to visit other countries
faire un apprentissage/devenir apprenti(e)	to do an apprenticeship/to become an apprentice
aller à l'université/continuer mes études à la fac(ulté)	to go to university/to continue my studies at university
faire du bénévolat/du travail bénévole	to do voluntary work
me marier ou me pacser	to get married or enter into a civil partnership
avoir des enfants	to have children
habiter/m'installer avec mon copain/ma copine	to live/move in with my boyfriend/girlfriend

Had a look ☐ **Nearly there** ☐ **Nailed it** ☐

Gagner de l'argent — Earning money

Tu as un petit boulot?	Do you have a part-time job?
Que fais-tu pour gagner de l'argent?	What do you do to earn money?
J'aide à la maison.	I help at home.
Je passe l'aspirateur.	I do the vacuuming.
Je fais la vaisselle.	I do the dishes.

Je lave la voiture (de mon père).	I wash the car (my dad's car).
Je tonds la pelouse (de mes grands-parents).	I mow the lawn (my grandparents' lawn).
Je promène le chien.	I walk the dog.
J'ai un petit boulot.	I have a part-time job.
Je sers les clients.	I serve customers.
Je remplis les rayons.	I stack the shelves.
Je fais du baby-sitting (pour mes voisins).	I babysit (for my neighbours).
Je livre des journaux.	I deliver newspapers.
Je gagne/Je reçois …	I earn/I receive/get …
Mon père/Ma mère me donne …	My father/mother gives me …
Mes parents me donnent …	My parents give me …
quinze euros/dix livres …	fifteen euros/ten pounds …
… par heure/jour/semaine/mois	… per hour/day/week/month

Had a look ☐ **Nearly there** ☐ **Nailed it** ☐

Postuler à un emploi — Applying for a job

une annonce	an advert
on recherche …	we are looking for …
les responsabilités (f)	responsibilities
les qualifications (f)	qualifications
les compétences (f)	skills
l'expérience (f)	experience
les atouts (m)	strengths
remplir un CV	to fill in a CV
écrire une lettre de motivation	to write a covering letter
faire une vidéo	to make a video

Had a look ☐ **Nearly there** ☐ **Nailed it** ☐

Mon stage — My work experience

J'ai fait un stage …	I did work experience …
dans un bureau	in an office
dans un garage	in a garage
dans un hôtel	in a hotel
dans un magasin de mode	in a clothes shop
dans un salon de coiffure	in a hairdressing salon
dans une banque	in a bank
J'ai servi les clients.	I served customers.
J'ai rangé les vêtements.	I tidied the clothes.
J'ai aidé les mécaniciens.	I helped the mechanics.
J'ai appris à changer des pneus.	I learned to change tyres.
J'ai tapé des documents.	I typed documents.
J'ai fait des photocopies.	I made photocopies.
J'ai lavé les cheveux des clients.	I washed customers' hair.
J'ai fait du café.	I made coffee.

M 7

41

J'ai passé l'aspirateur.	I did the vacuuming.
J'ai répondu au téléphone.	I answered the phone.
J'ai fait des réservations.	I made bookings.
J'ai envoyé des e-mails.	I sent emails.

Had a look ☐ **Nearly there** ☐ **Nailed it** ☐

C'était une bonne expérience?
Was it a good experience?

C'était ...	*It was ...*
amusant/bien	*fun/good*
génial/intéressant	*great/interesting*
passionnant	*exciting*
une bonne expérience	*a good experience*
difficile/ennuyeux	*difficult/boring*
fatigant/monotone	*tiring/monotonous*
(complètement) nul	*(completely) rubbish*
une mauvaise expérience	*a bad experience*
Mon patron/Ma patronne était ... gentil(le)/trop sévère.	*My boss was ... kind/too strict.*
Mes collègues (n') étaient (pas) (très) sympa.	*My colleagues were (not) (very) nice.*
J'ai beaucoup appris.	*I learned a lot.*
Je n'ai rien appris.	*I didn't learn anything.*

Had a look ☐ **Nearly there** ☐ **Nailed it** ☐

M 7

Extra words I should know for reading and listening activities

Les qualités personnelles / Personal qualities

Les qualités personnelles	Personal qualities
en bonne forme	fit
fort(e)/patient(e)	strong/patient
calme/sociable	calm/sociable
heureux/-euse	happy

Had a look ☐ **Nearly there** ☐ **Nailed it** ☐

L'avenir / The future

L'avenir	The future
un métier fascinant/passionnant	a fascinating/exciting job
Tu peux sauver la vie des gens!	You can save people's lives!
Tu peux devenir célèbre!	You can become famous!
Pourquoi ne pas devenir … ?*	Why not become … ?
Pense à être …	Think of being …
Aimerais-tu être … ?*	Would you like to be … ?
Je prendrai …	I will take …
J'irai …	I will go …
J'aurai …	I will have …
Je serai …*	I will be …
Je trouverai …	I will find …
Je me marierai …	I will get married …
l'homme/la femme de mes rêves	the man/woman of my dreams
ma propre entreprise	my own business
le tour du monde**	tour of the world
Ce sera génial!	It will be great!
le mariage	the marriage
la cérémonie	the ceremony
l'église (f)	the church
mon futur mari/ma future femme	my future husband/wife
être marié(e)(s) depuis … ans	to be married for … years
habiter ensemble	to live together
pour voir si ça marche	to see if it works out
fonder une famille	to start a family

Had a look ☐ **Nearly there** ☐ **Nailed it** ☐

> ⭐ *Remember **not** to use an article after a verb (conjugated or in the infinitive form) when you are talking about a job.
>
> Examples
>
> Pourquoi ne pas devenir pilote? — Why not become a pilot?
> Aimerais-tu être chanteuse? — Would you like to be a singer?
> Je serai prof. — I will be a teacher.
>
> Jobs in French usually have masculine and feminine versions of their spellings but not all.

Pour gagner de l'argent … / To earn money …

Pour gagner de l'argent …	To earn money …
Je fais ça gratuitement.	I do that for free.
chaque semaine	every week
quand il/elle n'est pas là	when he/she isn't there
J'ai déjà un peu d'expérience de …	I already have a little experience of …
postuler au poste de …	to apply for the post/position of …

Had a look ☐ **Nearly there** ☐ **Nailed it** ☐

Les expériences récentes / Recent experiences

Les expériences récentes	Recent experiences
J'ai travaillé …	I worked …
J'ai supervisé …	I supervised …
J'ai décidé de …	I decided to …
J'ai commencé à …	I started to …
Mon travail consiste à …	My job consists of …
Les horaires sont (un peu) longs.	The days/The working hours are (a little) long.

Had a look ☐ **Nearly there** ☐ **Nailed it** ☐

Le service civique / Civic service

Le service civique	Civic service
pour aider les autres	to help others
Ça consiste en/à …	It consists of …
une période de (six) à (douze) mois	a period of (six) to (twelve) months
selon (leurs) centres d'intérêt	according to (their) interests
choisir parmi un grand nombre de «missions»	to choose from a large number of 'missions'
la culture et les loisirs	culture and leisure
l'éducation et la santé	education and health
les sports ou l'environnement	sports or the environment
le point de départ	the starting point
trouver un emploi	to find a job
(leur) motivation principale	(their) main motivation
faire quelque chose d'utile à la société	to do something useful for society
(Le service civique) sera un atout pour (leur) CV.	(Civic service) will be a strength on (their) CV.

Had a look ☐ **Nearly there** ☐ **Nailed it** ☐

> ⭐ **Some nouns in French change their meaning, depending on whether they are used in the masculine or feminine form.
>
> le Tour de France — the Tour de France (cycle race)
> la tour Eiffel — the Eiffel Tower

M 7

Words I should know for speaking and writing activities

Ce qui est important pour moi / What's important to me

Ce qui est important pour moi, c'est …	What's important to me is …
l'argent (m)	money
le sport	sport
la musique	music
ma famille	my family
ma santé	my health
mes amis (m)	my friends
mes animaux (m)	my animals
mes études (f)	my studies

Had a look ☐ **Nearly there** ☐ **Nailed it** ☐

Ce qui me préoccupe / What concerns me

Ce qui me préoccupe, c'est …	What concerns me is …
l'environnement (m)	the environment
l'état (m) de la planète	the state of the planet
le racisme	racism
la cruauté envers les animaux	cruelty to animals
la faim	hunger
la guerre	war
l'injustice (f)	injustice
la pauvreté	poverty
la violence	violence

Had a look ☐ **Nearly there** ☐ **Nailed it** ☐

Qu'est-ce qu'on peut faire pour aider? / What can we do to help?

On peut faire du bénévolat.	You can do voluntary work.
On peut parrainer un enfant.	You can sponsor a child.
On peut donner de l'argent à une association caritative.	You can give money to a charity.
On peut recycler.	You can recycle.
Il faut agir.	You/We have to act.
Il faut lutter contre la faim.	You/We have to fight against hunger.
Il faut signer des pétitions.	You/We have to sign petitions.
Il faut participer à des manifestations.	You/We have to take part in demonstrations.
Il faut éduquer les gens.	You/We have to educate people.

Had a look ☐ **Nearly there** ☐ **Nailed it** ☐

Quel temps fera-t-il? / What will the weather be like?

Il y aura …	There will be …
de la pluie	rain
de la neige	snow
du vent	wind
du tonnerre	thunder
des averses (f)	showers
des éclairs (m)	lightning
des éclaircies (f)	sunny intervals
Il fera …	It/The weather will be …
beau	nice, good
mauvais	bad
chaud	hot
froid	cold
frais	chilly
Le temps sera …	The weather will be …
ensoleillé	sunny
nuageux	cloudy
orageux	stormy

Had a look ☐ **Nearly there** ☐ **Nailed it** ☐

Les problèmes environnementaux / Environmental problems

Le plus grand problème environnemental, c'est …	The biggest environmental problem is …
le changement climatique	climate change
le manque d'eau potable	the lack of drinking water
la disparition des espèces	the extinction of species
la destruction des forêts tropicales	the destruction of the rainforests
la surpopulation	overpopulation
la pollution de l'air	air pollution
la sécheresse	drought
les inondations (f)	flooding, floods
les incendies (m)	fires
Les arbres nous donnent de l'oxygène et nous les coupons tous les jours.	Trees give us oxygen, and every day we cut them down.
Beaucoup de personnes n'ont pas accès à cette ressource vitale.	Lots of people don't have access to this vital resource.
On détruit la planète.	We are destroying the planet.
C'est très inquiétant.	It's very worrying.
C'est catastrophique.	It's catastrophic.

Had a look ☐ **Nearly there** ☐ **Nailed it** ☐

Que doit-on faire pour sauver notre planète? / What should we do to save our planet?

On doit/On peut …	You/We should/can …
recycler	recycle
trier les déchets	separate/sort the rubbish
faire du compost	make compost

consommer moins d'énergie	consume less energy
éteindre les appareils électriques et la lumière	turn off electrical appliances and the light
mettre un pullover au lieu d'allumer le chauffage	put on a jumper instead of turning on the heating
faire des achats responsables	make responsible purchases
utiliser du papier recyclé	use recycled paper
acheter des produits verts et des produits bio	buy green and organic products

Had a look ☐ **Nearly there** ☐ **Nailed it** ☐

voyager autrement	travel differently
utiliser les transports en commun	use public transport
aller au collège à vélo	go to school by bike
réutiliser	reuse
refuser les sacs en plastique	turn down plastic bags
avoir une bouteille d'eau au lieu de prendre un gobelet jetable	have a bottle of water instead of taking a disposable cup
économiser l'eau	save water
boire l'eau du robinet	drink tap water
prendre une douche au lieu de prendre un bain	take a shower instead of a bath
tirer la chasse d'eau moins fréquemment	flush the toilet less frequently
fermer le robinet en se lavant les dents	turn off the tap while brushing your teeth
installer des panneaux solaires	install solar panels

Had a look ☐ **Nearly there** ☐ **Nailed it** ☐

D'où vient ton tee-shirt?
Where does your T-shirt come from?

Les produits pas chers sont souvent fabriqués dans des conditions de travail inacceptables.	Cheap products are often made in unacceptable working conditions.
Les ouvriers sont sous-payés.	The workers are underpaid.
Leur journée de travail est trop longue.	Their working day is too long.
Il faut/On doit …	We must …
forcer les grandes marques à garantir un salaire minimum	force big brands to guarantee a minimum wage
acheter des produits issus du commerce équitable	buy fair trade products
acheter des vêtements fabriqués en France/au Royaume-Uni	buy clothes that are made in France/in the UK

réfléchir à l'impact sur l'environnement	think about the impact on the environment
essayer de respecter l'homme et l'environnement à la fois	try to respect people and the environment at the same time

Had a look ☐ **Nearly there** ☐ **Nailed it** ☐

Faire du bénévolat
Doing volunteer work

Tu peux/J'aimerais …	You can/I would like …
travailler avec des personnes âgées	to work with elderly people
travailler avec des enfants	to work with children
travailler avec des sans-abri/des SDF	to work with homeless people
travailler avec des animaux	to work with animals
participer à un projet de conservation	to participate in a conservation project
Je fais du bénévolat parce que …	I do volunteer work because …
pour moi, c'est important d'aider les autres	for me, it's important to help other people
pour moi, c'est important de participer à la vie en société	for me, it's important to participate in society
j'aime développer de nouvelles compétences	I like developing new skills
j'aime rencontrer de nouvelles personnes	I like meeting new people
c'est une expérience enrichissante pour moi	it's a rewarding experience for me
ça me donne plus confiance en moi	it gives me more confidence in myself

Had a look ☐ **Nearly there** ☐ **Nailed it** ☐

Je travaille avec …	I work with …
J'aide un enfant avec ses devoirs.	I help a child with his homework.
Je participe à …	I participate in …
Je suis membre de l'organisation …	I am a member of the organisation …
Je travaille dans un refuge.	I work in a refuge/shelter.
Je parle/discute avec …	I talk to …
Je promène les chiens.	I walk the dogs.

Had a look ☐ **Nearly there** ☐ **Nailed it** ☐

Les grands événements
Big events

Cet événement/Ce genre d'événement …	This event/This type of event …
attire les touristes	attracts tourists

M 8

encourage la pratique du sport	*encourages participation in sport*
donne des modèles aux jeunes	*gives young people role models*
permet aux gens de s'amuser	*allows people to have a good time*
unit les gens	*unites people*
L'année dernière/L'été dernier, …	*Last year/Last summer, …*
je suis allé(e) à un festival/à la Coupe du Monde	*I went to a festival/to the World Cup*
j'ai vu (le Tour de France)	*I saw (the Tour de France)*
C'est …	*It's …*
un événement qui est connu dans le monde entier	*an event that is known throughout the world*
le plus grand festival (de théâtre) au monde	*the biggest (theatre) festival in the world*
Il y a une ambiance magique!	*There is a magical atmosphere!*
Il a lieu/Ça se passe (à Nice/en février).	*It takes place (in Nice/in February).*
L'été prochain/L'année prochaine, …	*Next summer/Next year, …*
je vais y retourner	*I am going to go back there*
je vais aller à …	*I am going to go to …*
je vais encore regarder …	*I am going to watch … again*

Had a look ☐ **Nearly there** ☐ **Nailed it** ☐

M
8

Extra words I should know for reading and listening activities

Le climat de notre planète	Our planet's climate
Il y aura (plus/moins de) soleil/pluie/vent/neige/tempêtes tropicales.	There will be (more/less) sun/rain/wind/snow/tropical storms.
un (très violent) cyclone/ouragan*	a (very violent) cyclone/hurricane
le changement climatique au cours du XXIe siècle	climate change over the course of the 21st century
la température globale	global temperature
les conséquences (f)	the consequences
causer d'énormes destructions et plusieurs morts	to cause massive destruction and several deaths
frapper	to strike, to hit
le Pacifique sud	the southern Pacific Ocean
contaminer	to pollute
une ressource vitale	a vital resource
recycler le verre/carton/papier	to recycle glass/cardboard/paper
allumer rarement le chauffage	to rarely put the heating on
être membre d'une équipe verte	to be a member of an environmental team
installer des panneaux solaires	to put in solar panels

Had a look ☐   Nearly there ☐   Nailed it ☐

Les produits verts?	Environmentally friendly products?
Le coton est cultivé …	The cotton is grown …
Le coton est une plante.	Cotton is a plant.
Les balles de coton sont transportées/chargées/exportées/transformées/envoyées …	The cotton balls are transported/loaded/exported/transformed/sent …
en tissu	into material

fabriquer dans une usine	to make in a factory
repartir pour	to set off back to
le motif	slogan
imprimé(e)	printed
Tu portes le tee-shirt pendant un moment …	You wear the T-shirt for a while …
Tu donnes le tee-shirt à une association caritative.	You give the T-shirt to a charity.
vendu à un prix favorable	sold at a good price
les gens dans les pays pauvres	people in poor countries
avoir quelque chose de qualité	to have something of quality
Évitons la pollution!**	Let's avoid pollution!

Had a look ☐   Nearly there ☐   Nailed it ☐

Le bénévolat	Voluntary work
planter des arbres	to plant trees
le froid	the cold
la solitude	loneliness

Had a look ☐   Nearly there ☐   Nailed it ☐

Les grands événements	Big events
Ce genre d'événement encourage la pratique du sport.	This kind of event encourages people to do sport.
le festival d'Édimbourg	the Edinburgh festival
deux années de suite	two years in a row

Had a look ☐   Nearly there ☐   Nailed it ☐

M 8

*Take extra care with words that are very similar to words in English, for example:

l'ouragan	hurricane
le vent	wind
le gel	frost

**The nous form of the verb in the imperative tense is often used to convey the idea of doing something collectively.

Évitons la pollution! Let's avoid pollution!

ISBN 978-1-292-17256-9

9 781292 172569 >